the down way up

D1720359

THE down way up

Tyndale House
Publishers, Inc.
Wheaton, Illinois

The ROY COMSTOCK Story
by Carole Gift Page

Photos on pages 6 and 221 by Bill Page.

For obvious reasons, the
names of gang members
have been changed in this
narrative.

Library of Congress Catalog
Card Number 78-64668
ISBN 0-8423-0674-9, paper
Copyright © 1979 by Tyndale
House Publishers, Inc.,
Wheaton, Illinois. All rights
reserved. First printing,
January 1979. Printed in the
United States of America

FOREWORD

Shortly after our marriage several years ago, my husband Bill introduced me to Roy and Wanda Comstock. Roy, a blond, strapping fellow of 6′ 3″, swung his arm around Bill's shoulder (my husband is a solid but compact 5′ 6″) and said, "This is the guy who's responsible for bringing me to the Lord. We were high school classmates when Bill witnessed to me. I gave him a hard time, even threatened to bash his head in, but he never gave up on me."

I learned that Bill was a vital part of the testimony Roy gave wherever he went to speak or to preach. Over the years I heard bits and pieces of Roy Comstock's story, and the more I heard, the more intrigued I became. His was an incredible odyssey, a painful, inspiring tale involving not just his own life, but many lives intertwined irrevocably by the complexities of emotion, conflict, and deep human need.

Several times Roy told me, "Someday I'm going to write a book about my life." But he never quite got around to it. Then after church one Sunday in November, 1976, as Roy, Wanda, Bill, and I sat eating together in a restaurant, Roy said to me, "Carole, it's too bad you don't have time to write my book."

I was silent a moment. Then I replied, "Maybe I do have time."

That was the beginning. Over the next year I lived Roy and Wanda's story; vicariously I experienced their struggles and witnessed the panorama of God's working in their lives. The more I delved into their backgrounds, the more absorbed I became in the fascinating network of circumstances that brought them to where they are today. In a curious, indescribable sense I came to feel myself woven into the fabric of the Comstock clan; I felt I knew them as well as I knew my own thoughts.

I am grateful that just as God used my husband Bill to show Roy the way to a transformed life in Jesus Christ, so God allowed me the privilege of giving life to Roy and Wanda's story.

Carole Gift Page
Garden Grove, California

PROLOGUE

He stands poised to spring. A razor-sharp sense of expectancy hones his muscles, his impulses, his perception. With a dry, acrid taste in his mouth, he waits suspended in a gesture of attack, motionless. It's taking too long. He should have been able to strike and be gone by now.

For one long paralyzing hour he has watched the house, his eyes riveted to the single muted light in an upstairs window. Someone's still up. He sees a silhouette appear, vanish, appear again. Blasted luck!

Swathed in shadows, his spine rigid from tension, he swings his gaze from the house to the car parked beside the curb. A tidy, baby blue Cadillac convertible. A real prize. Sure to bring in more than the usual two- or three-hundred dollar payoff. Much more.

The youth flinches involuntarily as the house is suddenly snuffed to darkness. *Lights out. Give yourself another ten minutes,* he orders severely. The words pulse with the blood rushing through his temples, almost an audible drumming in his brain.

He counts off minutes. Six . . . eight . . . ten. Then he moves. Soundlessly. Across the street. Caught momentarily by pale street light. Blue-white rays sweeping his cropped blond hair. A tall lean body. Angular features. Then shadows again. A figure pressing close to the gleaming automobile, a wire artfully inserted over the window, the lock snagged, lifted, the door opened noiselessly. *Five seconds.*

The youth strains briefly beneath the dashboard, pushing with deft fingers until his fine nail-like tool jams and connects. The engine turns over and purrs steadily. Door shut. Foot on the gas. The vehicle lurches forward. Engine roars, wheels sing over pavement.

She handles like a dream.

The youth settles back, the sweet excitement of success rising like adrenaline, working through his veins, almost tangible in the close perimeters of the automobile. He takes the corner with ease, flying high, then guns the engine and cruises effortlessly along Pioneer Boulevard.

With a studied carelessness he reaches over and flips on the radio. Fats Domino, in his slow, broken, gravelly drawl, fills the padded interior with the poignant lyrics of "Blueberry Hill."

Aloud, the youth tells himself, "Hey, Comstock, you're no loser tonight. You've got it made. Man, you're home free."

The scene blurs. Darkness evaporates into daylight. Sun rays stab with a splintered distortion, as if somehow viewed through a prism. Then objects take shape. A classroom slips into focus— chalkboard, maps, desks, students seated, supposedly attentive. A door. Someone enters. The instructor pauses in mid-sentence. A stern-faced man in a business suit approaches, and in a confidential monotone, questions, "Is Roy Comstock here?"

With a nod and a slight, baffled gesture in Roy's direction, the teacher replies, "That's Roy."

The man turns toward the youth, his face expressionless. "Would you come with me, please?"

Roy Comstock eases out of his seat and stretches to his full height. Silently he follows the man out of the room and down the hall to the principal's office. Mr. Hastings is seated at his desk, a frown creasing his brows. Mr. Atkins, Dean of Boys, stands beside the desk, his face grim. He is the one man who has believed in Roy and encouraged him. "I know there has to be some mistake here, Roy," he says, conveying more concern than reassurance.

Another man stands beside Mr. Atkins. From his pocket he removes a wallet and opens it perfunctorily to reveal a badge.

"Police officer," he murmurs. Then, fastening his gaze on the youth, he declares, "Roy Comstock, you are under arrest. You have been charged with ten counts of auto theft."

A chill prickles Roy's skin. He feels stunned, as if he has been slapped with ice water. Standing rigid, speechless, his jaw stiff, he cannot force his muscles to act against the deadening cold. He cannot react. Not for fifteen years has he felt such coldness numbing his bones. It's almost a physical ache.

CHAPTER ONE

Cold.

He was distressingly cold—inescapably cold. The damp chill had seeped into his bones and lodged there, a bitter, unshakable presence.

He was hungry too. The gnawing ache never went away, not even now when there were plenty of potatoes and lumpy Dick— the tasteless flour-and-water mixture that had become a staple of life for the Comstock family.

Roy was not yet three years old. The memories he would carry with him of this time and place would be dim, disjointed— the fragments of recollections like bits of glass in a kaleidoscope, moving, changing, always elusive. Nevertheless, they would leave an indelible impression.

Until this year, Roy had been the baby in the family. He and Ray. The twins. No one ever said, "Where's Roy? What's Roy doing?" Rather: "Where are the twins? Someone get the twins."

The two of them were inseparable—towheaded imps, playing together in the dirt and mud with old tires, battered army boots, empty tin cans, or whatever they could find in the nearby junk pile. And at night they slept together on bed rolls in the tent, snuggling close for warmth. Everyone slept together in the tent.

This year—the fall of 1941—Roy and Ray were "big boys," and Johnnie was the baby. Johnnie—tiny, bald, and squalling—had come to live with Roy's family on Christmas day, nine months ago. Sometimes Roy stood and stared at him in his crib. He watched Johnnie's tiny hands embrace the air when he cried, and clutch the narrow crib slats when he was happy. Roy liked watching Johnnie, liked the little puckered faces he made when he was hungry or wet. Whenever Roy put his hand inside the crib, Johnnie grasped his finger—sometimes so hard it hurt.

Often Momma sat in the rocking chair near the black potbellied stove and rocked the baby in her arms. She always sat bundled in a blanket or a shawl. Like a mother hen, she seemed to envelop Johnnie with her body, shutting out the cold. Over and over, in a high, soft singsong voice, she would murmur his name. *Johnniejohnniejohnnie.*

Over and over she crooned while the old rocking chair creaked back and forth on the uneven floor. From his nest in her arms Johnnie watched her and blew bubbles with his round, pink lips or made happy cooing sounds. Or he slept while Momma sat, trancelike, rocking for hours.

Sometimes Roy climbed into her lap too and put his face next to Johnnie's round fuzzy head. These were the only times Roy almost began to feel warm. And sometimes he dozed while his mother crooned her gentle lullaby.

> *Sleep, my baby, sleep.*
> *Johnnie, Johnnie, sleep.*

But Johnnie hadn't come to stay for very long.

Home for the Comstock family was a sprawling migrant camp near Merrill, Oregon, just north of the California border. Dirt everywhere. Shanties, shacks, and tents formed haggard lines over the brown landscape, carving vague boundaries for makeshift roads on the hard, rutted ground. Only an occasional dilapidated automobile or sagging flatbed truck broke the long rows of shelters.

Women in loose-fitting, cotton print dresses hung clothing on lines tied from tent to shack or from shanty to tree. Children mulled about, squint-eyed, their expressions settled into permanent frowns—the look of hunger, of boredom. Cars rumbled over the ground, their engines roaring with a choking ferocity.

Dust followed on their tails like dark phantoms, rising in huge billowing swirls that colored the air brown.

At night the men returned wearily from the fields, still sweating even though the weather had turned cold. Every morning Howard Comstock left his tent (a big brown army surplus tent—actually two tents placed end to end) while it was still pitch black outside. He did not return until long after sundown. He ate one meal a day, after work in the evening. It was enough. Who had time to think of food?

This night, a night in late September, he returned to the tent and found potatoes, gravy, bread, butter, and coffee on the table. "Butter?" he grunted approvingly. "Ain't seen butter in weeks."

"It sure beats lumpy Dick," said Bill, the eight-year-old who already had his father's rugged good looks.

Bertha Comstock poured coffee into a mug and pushed it toward her husband. In a gesture that she used often, unconsciously, she pulled her shawl closer around her shoulders. "So damp tonight," she murmured. But her words were more like a sigh which her husband seemed not to hear.

The baby whimpered.

"Bring him here, Milt," she told the boy who held the infant. Milt, her oldest son, almost twelve, round-faced and curly headed, put Johnnie in her arms. "This baby don't eat enough to keep a flea alive," she said in a high, soft, complaining voice. She settled into the rocker and the whimpering subsided.

"We got milk, don't we?" said Howard.

"Just barely."

"Well, we'll get what we need."

"He don't drink it anyway."

"Is he sick?"

"I don't know."

The man drained his coffee cup and wiped his mouth with the back of his hand. "You going with me out to the spud yard tomorrow?"

"Momma's sick, " said Pansy, reaching for a piece of bread. She was seven, the oldest daughter except for Eulah. But no one talked about Eulah. It was possible no one even thought about her anymore, except Momma.

"Sick? Who says Momma's sick?" her husband asked gruffly.
"She was in bed all day," said Milt. "Just got up to fix supper."
"You coulda done that, Milt. I pay you—"
"I *told* Ma I'd fix supper."
"Well, I ain't sick. So there."
"You're too sick to work in the spud yards," Milt told her.
Bertha stroked the cheek of her sleeping child. "It ain't fair for
Milt to have the full responsibility. He can't ever go off with his
friends or have a time of his own."
"What do you think I pay him fifty cents a day for? To take
care of things while we're in the field. He's got his job, same as
we do."
Bertha lowered her head until her thin, pursed lips touched
the infant's brow. "Milt's a good boy. Works so hard. He's a
good boy, ain't he, Johnnie?"
Howard Comstock pushed back his chair and rubbed his large
hands on his overalls. "It's been a while. Maybe we should have
us a family meetin'. Last time was summer when we was in
Salem workin' the hops fields."
"What we gonna talk about?" asked Pansy, pushing back a
strand of wispy brown hair that had slipped loose from a white
plastic barrette.
"Get yourselves around the stove and we'll see what's to talk
about."
The children scurried about, laughing and pushing playfully. It
was exciting when Dad called a family conference. They settled
unceremoniously around the black potbellied stove that occupied
the middle of the tent. Bill and Richard sat off to one side,
surreptitiously punching each other in the ribs. Pansy and Joy
curled up on their bedrolls closest to the stove's smoky heat.
The twins nuzzled against Milt like drowsy pups.
Their father leaned forward, his features sharpened by the
orange glow of the kerosene lamp on the table. Resting his solid
forearms on his knees, he stared momentarily at his hands.
Absently he worked with the dirt under one thumbnail. Gazing
at the twins nestled in Milt's arms, his expression softened. "The
twins—and sure, Johnnie too—don't know what all's goin' on
here—the work we're doin', the things we got starin' us in the
face. The rest of us knows. The cold's comin' and there's not
enough food sometimes, and we work from sunup to sunset and

don't get nowhere. That's how it looks. But we're makin' it. You twins don't pay no mind to this stinkin' tent and the cold and the dirt and the potatoes stacked like kindling. We're gonna be OK."

Bill stopped poking Richard long enough to ask, "When's things gonna change, so we don't hafta live like this no more?" Milt spoke up too. "How long we got to keep movin', followin' the crops?"

A flicker of irritation crossed the man's face. His jaw hardened and the words came out guttural. "It's these times we're in, boy. The war. Why, look how it's affected the crops—cut down on exports and all. That's what they tell us, anyways. Look how the government's had to give the farmers a hand, keep 'em from fallin' on their faces." He looked from Bill to Milt. "But it's not just this war. We been down since the depression. You didn't know it like I did—the way it hit like a whirlwind and knocked you down. Took everything. Left you stunned. You never saw what it did to a man."

"Is that why we're poor, Daddy?" Pansy asked softly.

"We're better off'n some," her father shot back. The harshness faded almost immediately. "This life's not what I'd pick for you, Pansy Mae, but we ain't gonna blubber about it neither. We'll do what we gotta do."

Pansy chewed thoughtfully on a strand of hair. "Daddy, I heard this girl . . . this girl . . . she said we was white trash. Are we, Daddy?"

The veins in Howard Comstock's temples constricted, protruding slightly beneath the skin. His eyes grew flinty, flashing a peculiar light all their own. "Don't you use them words to me again, daughter. And don't you let no one call you that, never in your life, Pansy Mae, you hear?"

He stood up and inhaled sharply. Then, slowly, he expelled his breath. It sounded loud in the dead silence of the tent. After a moment he reached out and rumpled Pansy's hair; then he turned to Milt and gathered the sleeping twins into his arms. Roy's head lopped against his father's shoulder, but he didn't stir.

Front row: Ray, Pansy, Roy, Joy
Back row: Bill, Richard, Father, Johnny, Mother, Milt

19

CHAPTER TWO

"Hold still," said Milt with mock sternness. The twins squirmed
out of his grasp, laughing. Milt reached out and caught Roy's
arm. "Come here. I'm gonna make you another Joe Louis." He
took a sock and stuffed it with rags, pulled it over Roy's left
hand, and tied it. He tugged another rag-stuffed sock on to Roy's
right hand. The child shook his swaddled hands gleefully.

Milt stuffed two more socks and slipped them over Ray's
hands, tying them firmly at the wrist. "Go to it now," he told the
twins, coaxing them toward each other. "Come on, you got on
boxing gloves. Let's see you two box."

Ray, wearing a frayed coat several sizes too large, raised a
sock-cushioned fist and swung awkwardly at Roy. Missed. He
toppled. Then scrambled to his feet. But Roy was already
pushing forward with both fists raised—straight for Ray. Before
Roy could strike, Ray shot his fist toward his brother. Roy
recoiled as Ray's fist made contact. He began to whimper. Milt
pushed Roy toward his twin, and the two boys scuffled briefly.
Then the game was old, so they scuttled back to Milt and
pounced artlessly on him.

Milt scooped up the youngsters, chuckling with amusement.
"You guys're OK. No one's gonna walk over you!" He stood up
and brushed dirt from his overalls. "You two go play. I gotta go
empty the honey buckets."

He trudged back to the tent and went inside, stepping up on

the creaking wooden platform that served as a floor. Only this tent had a floor; the tent where they slept sat directly on the ground. It wasn't so bad when the weather was good, but now with the rainy season on them, there was no way to keep water from seeping under the tent, turning the dirt to mud. Milt had heard his dad talking to another man about the floors and about getting the tents ready for winter. The company had promised to put floors in both tents, but only one floor had been put in. And here it was almost October.

Milt went straight back to where the bedrolls lay. He pulled off urine-soaked sheets and took the bedpans—those reeking honey buckets—out from under his parents' brass bed. This bed and the solid wood table were the only large pieces of furniture they had brought with them from Grandpa Comstock's house up in Salem. Dad had inherited the house from Grandpa, then lost it when he couldn't pay the taxes.

Milt went outside and emptied the bedpans, then stretched the wet, yellowed sheets over the outside of the tent to dry in the sun. Not that there was much sun today. Its rays scarcely penetrated the gathering rain clouds.

Wash the sheets that the younger children soaked each night? There was no way to do it. Milt could only hang them out each morning, let them dry, and spread them back over the makeshift mattresses each night. Between the damp Oregon weather and the wet bedding, everything in the tent was mildewed. In fact, Milt could barely stomach the pungent, fetid odor that permeated the tents. But there was no way to dissipate the stench that hung oppressively over everything. He could only live with it.

But Milt, who slept between Bill and Richard, drew the line whenever *he* woke up wet. He always beat the tar out of the two of them for *that*.

Milt went back inside to find the twins delighting themselves in an overturned sack of sugar—attacking the sweet white mounds with an ecstasy that might have amused Milt, had not sugar been so scarce and so expensive. He yanked the twins away from their forbidden treasure and sent them skittering outside. After doing what he could to salvage the spilled contents, he bounded after the twins and forced soap into their mouths. "You like sugar so much, OK, how d'ya like the taste of this?"

Watching their shocked, puckered expressions, he felt a fleeting twinge of conscience. But he reminded himself that he was only doing his job. While his folks worked the fields, he had to be both mom and dad. If they were going to learn right from wrong, it was up to him to teach them.

Milt's thoughts were interrupted by Pansy and Joy returning from the camp exchange.

"Look at the dress Joy got," exclaimed Pansy, her voice light and breathless. "Don't it look bran' new?"

Five-year-old Joy Bell turned and pirouetted proudly in her green velvet dress. Never had she worn a dress like this before. It was a perfect fit, and, oh, as soft as old Tom Cat's yellow fur.

Bill joined Milt in marveling over his little sister. "Purtiest sight I ever seen. You look good enough to go out on the town!"

Milt laughed. "What you gonna do? Take her into Merrill?"

"No, but I know some folks havin' a birthday party tonight. Across the field. Joy Bell, I'm takin' you to a swell party. What d'ya thinka that?"

The child squealed. Pansy gave her a hug and said, "I'll fix your hair real pretty, Joy Bell. Right after lunch, OK?"

Milt boiled flour and water and salt on the potbellied stove to make lumpy Dick for lunch. He saved the potatoes, bread, and butter for evening when Momma and Dad would come in, tired and hungry. When Momma wasn't sick, she went with Dad every morning, joining the other pickers for a full day's work.

Dad was a foreman, a "pusher," and it was his job to supervise the pickers. After the windrows had been plowed, the pickers stooped along the furrows and collected the potatoes in big burlap sacks. Then a stitcher came along and closed the sack tops. Finally, men threw the sacks into horse-drawn wagons. Dad supervised the whole process.

Milt wished his mother didn't have to work those spud yards, dragging heavy sacks all day. She just wasn't up to it. A gentle woman, soft and delicate, she was not cut out for such labor. She should have been home raising her children. Then Milt would be free. But he felt guilty thinking this, thinking of freedom. Freedom was only a dream—a dream he dared not indulge in too often.

After the older children had eaten, Milt propped Johnnie in his lap and spoon-fed him the watery flour mixture. Johnnie pushed the stuff out of his mouth as quickly as Milt spooned it in. Before long his shirt front was soaked. Milt pulled the garment off over Johnnie's head.

Pansy came and sat down beside Milt. "Look, you can count his ribs," she said, reaching out and running her finger over Johnnie's chest.

Milt nodded. He noticed that Pansy looked concerned.

"He's been sneezing," she added. "Maybe he's got a cold."

"Could be." Milt wiped off Johnnie's mouth and put him back in his crib.

"Hey, Milt," called Richard, pushing open the tent flap. "Someone outside wants you." In a whisper he added, "You know, the one with them big fat cigars."

Milt went outside and greeted his burly, cigar-puffing neighbor. The man gripped the cigar between his teeth while he talked. It bobbed up and down with every syllable. Milt had to strain to understand him.

"Jus' took ma missus inta da hospital," he told Milt. "Thought mebbe yer folks'd wanta know."

"What's wrong with her?"

"Looks like pneumonia. Thas what da camp doctor sez."

"That right?"

"Sez a slew a folks been comin' down wi' somethun. Mebbe pneumonia. Climate here don' help none." The smell of beer was strong on the man's breath. Milt figured he must have found time to stop off somewhere. Or maybe, like some of the men in camp, he carried his own bottle.

"My ma's been sick some, but that's normal," said Milt, to make conversation.

"Well, yer ma's right lucky to have you," said the man. "Yer a good kid to do all ya do fer yer folks. Wish ma sons was like you. Thar plain lazy."

Milt gestured toward the tent. "You want some coffee? I can fix it quick."

The man shook his head, took his cigar between his fingers and spat from the side of his mouth. "Naw, I got double duty, wi' ma missus sick." He eyed Milt for a moment and grinned. "Any time ya wanta work ma place . . . there's lots to do." He stabbed his cigar back between his teeth and shuffled away.

Bertha Comstock came home early from the field. The minute Milt saw her he felt a knot in his stomach. She walked as if she could scarcely drag herself along, as if her body were dead weight. Milt met her and took her arm. Her skin felt hot in spite of the chill wind.

"You got a fever, Momma?"

"Maybe. Thought I was gonna faint dead away out there."

"We better get you to bed. Man down the way sez his wife's got pneumonia. Sez it's goin' round."

Milt helped his mother into the tent. Joy Bell stood there in her new green velvet dress, her face glowing. To Milt she looked like a Christmas angel.

"Bill's takin' me to a birthday party in my new dress," she told her mother in a soft, pleased voice.

"You look mighty purty, child," Bertha said, twisting her lips into a smile.

Bill sauntered in then and took Joy by the hand. "Wait'll them folks see you!" he whistled. Then he led her across the field to the birthday party place.

It rained that evening. Torrents. Drenched everything. Bill and Joy came back soaking wet, moaning and shivering. Joy's dress was dripping pools around her feet. The velvet was caked with mud. Joy bawled so hard no one could tell her tears from the rivulets streaming from her sopping-wet hair.

"There wasn't even no birthday party," Bill complained loudly, pulling off his wet boots. "We stayed anyway. Didn't figure on havin' to wade through a muddy field."

Dad came in carrying an armload of potatoes. He stacked them against one side of the tent. His shirt was so wet it stuck to his back and his hat had been battered shapeless by the downpour. "Hey, Curly, I got us plenty of potatoes to bake," he told Milt.

"Dad, Momma's sick in bed. She can't get warm no matter how she bundles up," said Milt, almost in one breath. "But her head, it feels like it's on fire."

Howard Comstock took off his hat and coughed harshly. He pulled a wrinkled handkerchief from his overalls pocket and mopped his face. He coughed again, deep from his chest. "Everyone's comin' down," he mumbled. "Whole camp. The rains don't help. You tend to the youngsters, Milt. I'll get your Momma another blanket."

Back in a moment, he said sternly, "Milt, come help me push Momma's bed out here by the stove. She's shivering herself to pieces."

Around midnight, Milt woke to find himself wet, but this time it wasn't Bill or Richard's fault. Rain water was seeping in under the tent.

He got up quietly and checked on his mother in her new spot by the stove. Asleep, she looked peaceful, her face relaxed like he never saw it during the day. Dad was sleeping soundly beside her.

Milt was about to return to bed when, without warning, his brothers and sisters swarmed out of their sleeping quarters, clutching their bedrolls in their arms.

"The tent's flooded," gasped Richard.

"It's a river of mud," exclaimed Pansy.

"I'm freezing," sobbed Joy.

Pushing the kerosene lamp to one side, they stacked their wet bedding on the table.

The twins, groggy from sleep, wrapped mud-streaked arms around Milt's neck and whimpered softly. Milt heard his father cough and stir. He waited expectantly, but his father was silent again. Milt looked around in dismay from one cold, trembling youngster to another. All were waiting for his solution. On one hand he wanted to gather them all in his arms to protect them from the misery. On the other hand, he wanted to turn and run.

CHAPTER THREE

"Johnnie is sick."

"She don't hear you."

"Momma, do you hear me? Johnnie is sick. Got diarrhea real bad."

"Look at her. She don't even know what you're sayin'."

Milt and Bill's voices. She did hear them, heard every word. But she just couldn't respond, couldn't bring herself to focus on the meaning of their words. Their voices sounded hollow, like faint echoes.

She too was sick. Had to be, to feel like this, so severed from everything. Perhaps this feeling would pass and the world would come into focus, take shape, become real again.

Perhaps if she recited familiar things. Her name: Bertha Louise Comstock. Once her name had been Armstrong, but that was long ago, in Cleveland. She remembered her mother—Phebe Sophia Ensign Armstrong. A wealthy woman, what they called aristocratic looking, an elegant lady. But that was only at first—before she married Bertha's father. Phebe's parents had disinherited her for that.

Bertha strained her memory. She couldn't recall her father. Of course not. He died when she was two. Her mother worked as a seamstress to support four children. Bertha was the baby. Her brother was fourteen years older than she, her sisters nine and ten years older. How they pampered and protected her! Such sweet, carefree days. No one had prepared her for the sort of life she lived now. But then no one had prepared Howard either. Bertha forced her mind to concentrate on her husband. Howard Orville Comstock. A nice strong name. He came from Nebraska. Strikingly handsome, he was tall, solidly built, with curly brown hair, a strong jaw and manly, chiseled features. Howard had swept her off her feet right from the start.

But he too had once been the baby, pampered just as much as she by sisters fourteen and fifteen years older. No one had taught either of them how to force an existence out of hard, unyielding land. The depression hit about the time they married, snatching what little they had. And then the children came— eight in almost as many years (nine if she counted Eulah), each demanding more of Bertha than she had to give.

Bertha herself wasn't a bad looking woman, at least not before the children came along. Howard had found her attractive. Somewhere she had a photograph of herself that showed a young woman with a full oval face, dark, almond-shaped eyes, and thick brows feathering out lightly toward her temples. She had a small chin, a full, graceful neck, and thin, pursed lips. Her skin looked smooth as cream and her dark brown hair was cropped becomingly around her face. Now, of course, her middle had thickened a bit, her features sagged, and her hair was tied back severely.

Today Bertha was aware of another face nudging her consciousness, but the image remained a blur. She couldn't quite place it. Perhaps her first husband? A man named Jewett, a vague shadow of a man she had long since forgotten.

No. It was not his face she saw, but a child's. Eulah Marie's.

Bertha heard a cry. Someone shouting Eulah's name. Who cried?

Then someone said insistently, "Momma! Momma, are you OK?"

Bertha opened her eyes and stared into Milt's ashen face. His eyes were wide, startled. "You must've had a nightmare," he told her. "You were shoutin'."

"I'm all right," she murmured. She laid her head back. So, it had been her own voice she heard, her own cry. She felt exhausted.

"You want somethin' to eat, Momma? Maybe some coffee?"

She shook her head. "Water."

Milt disappeared momentarily and returned with a cup of tepid water. He propped her up while she drank.

"You been asleep all day," he said. "The twins and Joy and Richard got the runs now. What with no place to wash, I just took off their underpants and let them run naked."

"J—Johnnie?"

"He's fretful, Momma. Everything goes right through him. His little bottom's red as a beet."

Bertha closed her eyes. She had no strength to talk. She would go to Johnnie, try to help him. But she could hardly raise her head. Besides, the other child's face was still there, before her closed eyelids. Eulah—dark curly hair, red cheeks, plump, beautiful. Bertha's first child. Only two years old. Gone. Gone . . . how long? Over twelve years now?

Did it really happen? Did someone really steal her child, make her disappear off the face of the earth? How could it be? Bertha still recalled the day, that terrible day—how she left her baby with a nice couple, good, God-fearing people. People she thought were her friends. They had seemed so kind, so concerned. That day Bertha had gone out. Hours later she came back. There was no one in the house. The couple was gone. Eulah was gone. The police would find nothing, no leads. How could a baby disappear like that? It was as if the child had never existed.

Bertha felt a familiar oppressiveness, the weight of grief. Her lost child tugged at her heart day and night, leaving an ache that nothing else could fill. The memory was vivid even now as slumber softened Bertha's expression and relaxed the knots of tension in her fingers.

Quietly Milt approached his mother's bedside. Thank goodness, she was sleeping soundly. How many times these last few days had she drifted between fitful slumber and uneasy wakefulness? Her condition refused to improve. Her fever persisted.

Now the other youngsters were sick too. Johnnie was sicker than the rest. Milt wondered fleetingly if the child might be coming down with pneumonia. It didn't seem likely.

Actually, Milt himself didn't feel too well. But he didn't dare get sick. What with Momma sick in bed and Dad in the fields all

day, the full weight of the family was on his shoulders. There
was too much to do, too many responsibilities. He already felt as
if his hands were tied. How he hated that feeling of helplessness.

The recurring messes turned his stomach. The stench had
been bad enough before. But now! The fifty cents was no longer
worth the misery. If only he could get away, for just a few hours,
to breathe fresh air, to sort out his thoughts.

Maybe he *could! Tomorrow!* Yes, tomorrow he would just
take off by himself. Then he'd get back in time to tend to
everyone before Dad came home. Pansy could care for Momma
and watch Johnnie. She was big enough.

Milt left early the next morning. He planned to be back before
nightfall. But it was hard to surrender his brief freedom. He
dreaded returning to the dank atmosphere of the tents. Yet he
had no choice.

The moment he stepped back inside, he knew something was
wrong. The place was messier than ever. The children were
crying. Pansy, with tears running down her cheeks, rocked
Johnnie in her arms. "He's awful sick," she sobbed.

Milt's heart sank as his eyes scanned the twins sitting in their
own mess, Johnnie whimpering weakly, and Joy huddled,
shivering, on her bedroll by the stove. Before he could decide
where to turn his attention first, his father came in, looked
around, and grunted surprise. Milt could tell by his expression—
the way his eyes glinted and his nostrils flared—that he was
angry.

"What's going on here?"

Milt felt his mouth go dry. He licked his lips, but it didn't help.

"I asked a question, Milt. What's goin' on? Why's this place
such a mess and everyone cryin'?"

"J—Johnnie's sick. The others too," Milt blurted.

His father entered the other tent and came back grinding his
jaw. "The honey buckets ain't even been emptied. I guess you
didn't earn your fifty cents today, did you!"

Milt felt cut in half. Avoiding his father's disapproving gaze, he
collected the bedpans and went outside. He emptied the buckets
promptly but took his time returning to the tents. His insides
were churning, seething. Why did he feel such anger, such shame?
The two feelings collided in his chest, causing physical pain.

Back inside, he saw that his father's attention had been diverted. He was absorbed now with Johnnie, bending over the crib, feeling the child's forehead. "We better get the doctor here tomorrow," he said, his voice hoarse, unnatural. "I'll go fetch him myself if I have to."

The next morning Milt brought in wood and stooped beside the old black stove. "Sure cold out," he whistled as he stuffed wood into the stove's belly. "There's white frost all over everything."

Bill looked up from the potatoes he was slicing. "Dad should be back with the doctor by now, shouldn't he?"

"Should be. Must be lots of other camp people sick. How's Johnnie?"

Bill put down the potatoes, rubbed his hands on the front of his bib overalls, peered into Johnnie's crib. "He don't look good, Milt."

"No wonder. He don't eat nothin'. What he does eat goes straight through him."

"M—maybe he's starvin' to death."

"Shut your mouth!" Milt glanced out the tent flap and heaved a sigh of frustration. "Where's that doctor anyway?"

Dad arrived with the camp doctor within the hour. It took the weary-eyed physician only a few minutes of examination to pronounce ominously, "This baby belongs in the hospital."

Things happened quickly after that. Bertha Comstock, weak as she was, rallied enough to tell her husband she too would accompany Johnnie to the hospital. Pansy helped her mother dress. Milt wrapped Johnnie in layers of blankets. Then all the children gathered outside to wave goodbye as their folks climbed into their 1936 Reo sedan with Johnnie and drove away.

Even after the wheezing automobile rumbled out of sight, they all stood watching, waiting.

"He's already dead, I just know it," Bill mumbled under his breath.

Milt punched him in the shoulder. "Don't ever let me hear you say that again!"

Milt was in charge of the household. In *full* charge, with his parents so far away. For lunch he fried potatoes, using lard in the black cast-iron skillet. The children sat around the table, picking at their food in silence, except for the twins, who kept asking, "Where's Johnnie?"

It was dark before Dad returned. His expression was gloomy, preoccupied. His lips formed a severe line. He came in alone.

"Where's Momma?" asked Bill.

"She stayed. To be near Johnnie."

"How is he?" said Milt.

His father looked him in the eye. "Not good. Doc says he's got pneumonia. So much dirt in his lungs they call it 'dirt pneumonia.' Said he's suffering from malnutrition too."

"But we fed him."

"Not what he shoulda had."

"He'll be OK, won't he?"

His father didn't answer. He took some potatoes from the stove. Between bites he said, "I'll work the spud yards tomorrow and go to the hospital afterward. You won't see me here till late."

The next few days were long for everyone, especially Milt. He himself was fighting off the sickness. With lower temperatures every day, the sheets he hung outside became so stiff and cold the children refused to lie on them. And mornings were so bitter he thought the honey buckets would freeze over.

At the hospital the nurses fixed a place for Bertha Comstock to sleep. Each night when Howard came home the children clamored to know when Momma and Johnnie would be back. Each evening he put them off with a cryptic, "Wait and see."

On the third day, Howard came in directly from the fields. He saw that Joy Bell was too sick to eat. Her breathing was labored. He looked tiredly at Milt and said, "Get her ready, Curly. I'm taking her with me to the hospital."

Milt watched silently as his father drove away with Joy. A peculiar sense of aloneness swept over him. First Johnnie, now Joy. His family seemed to be falling apart before his eyes. His folks had always had rough times, but the family had hung together, working and sleeping side by side, buoying one another up when spirits sagged. Now some strange sickness was threatening the one good thing they had always possessed: family unity.

The evening hours dragged by. Milt waited up alone. Staring

into the flickering light of the kerosene lamp, he had no way to tell time. He'd wait up all night if he had to. Finally he heard the guttural roar of his father's old sedan. When he sprang to his feet and ran outside he was surprised to see his mother climb out of the car. She scuffed toward him. Momentarily the moonlight caught her face. Her expression chilled him. His father joined them and they went inside.

"Johnnie's dead," his father said matter-of-factly.

Milt wasn't ready for this. "He can't be," he argued. "He couldn't just *die!*" He looked at his mother. She hadn't moved.

Milt turned away. He had to hold on, had to stay in control. In spite of his resolves, his words erupted in anguish. "It's my fault. I shoulda taken better care of him. You were right, Dad. I didn't earn my fifty cents. It's because of me that Johnnie died!"

His father's rebuke was staggering. "You didn't have nothing to do with Johnnie's death! He just wasn't strong enough, that's all. It wasn't your fault. It wasn't nobody's fault. He just died, and that's the way it is."

Unexpectedly, Milt's mother took him in her arms. He flinched, startled. He couldn't remember her ever embracing him before. He blinked, struggling to keep back tears. He refused to let his parents see him cry.

"Johnnie's been sick a long while," she told him gently. "We done the best we could, all of us."

He felt her sag against him. Suddenly she seemed small and helpless. She hunched forward, her chin lost in her long, full neck. "My babies," she murmured distractedly. "Both my babies. My oldest and now my youngest. *Gone.* Eulah Marie. John Edward. My first child and my last . . . ."

Milt's father cleared his throat loudly. "Bertha? You OK?"

"Momma!" said Milt. He shook her gently.

"Both my babies gone . . . ."

Milt looked quizzically at his father.

Howard Comstock shook his head wearily. "This is hitting her hard, Curly." He took out his handkerchief and coughed into it, then said, "You know about the baby she lost years ago—the girl that was kidnapped. I thought maybe after all this time . . . but I guess your Momma never forgot."

Milt stared incredulously at his mother. "That's what she

means about the first and the last, the oldest and the youngest?"
He felt a wave of emotion, like nausea, hit him hard. He turned
abruptly and fled out of the tent.

He ran blindly. Ran until his lungs seemed about to burst.
Until spasms of pain tore at his sides, doubling him over.
Somewhere he collapsed on cold loamy ground, buried his head
in his hands and sobbed. Everything inside him revolted. With
his fists he punched the frozen earth until his knuckles throbbed.
His mind screamed accusations: *God in heaven, it isn't fair! If
we didn't have to live like this, Johnnie wouldn't be dead. If I
killed him, then we all killed him, by living like animals!*

Then he raised his face to the sky and said aloud, "Why were
we even born? Oh, God, if things had been different, Johnnie
would still be alive!"

CHAPTER FOUR

In years to come, only Pansy, among the Comstock children, would recall a few vague details of Johnnie's funeral. A hard narrow bench. A tiny coffin. A gravesite in Klamath Falls, Oregon. That was all.

In the days immediately following the funeral, Bertha Comstock took solace in her living children. Gathering them about her, she diverted their thoughts and hers by making up little games. She played red rover and hide-and-go-seek and London Bridge is falling down. She even squatted with her youngsters to make mud pies. It was as though she had become a child again.

But in the long black hours of the night the children would awaken to hear their mother weeping softly in her bed.

Five-year-old Joy Bell eventually returned from the hospital, recovered from pneumonia. Like the twins, she couldn't comprehend what had happened to Johnnie. Why was his crib no longer in the tent? Why did he go away? When would he come back? In one breath Joy would quiz her mother about Johnnie; in the next breath she'd tell the twins again about her hospital stay. Like the others, little Joy had faced her own frightening battle and survived, somehow stronger than before.

Years later, Roy Comstock would feel that in one way or another every member of his family was a victim of their painful years of poverty, illness, and death. Several of the children— including Roy—developed rickets which would plague them all of their lives. Young Richard contracted rheumatic fever and, in 1967, died of an enlarged heart. Milt, unable to shake his burden of guilt over Johnnie's death, began to run away from home, sometimes for two or three days at a time, and eventually for good.

As Bertha Comstock slipped farther into a state of depression and isolation, her husband grew more restless. At last he decided it was time to move; time to break with the miserable way of life his family had lived for a year—following the crops, moving from tenement to tent, often cold, sick, hungry. There had to be something better.

He'd find new work. In the past he'd worked in sawmills and lumber yards; he'd chased wild horses and broken them in for fifteen dollars a head; he'd worked on WPA building toilets; he'd even helped construct a Japanese concentration camp in California. There were other jobs. Somewhere he'd find one.

One evening Howard gathered his wife and children around the stove for another family conference. "It's time we figured what we're gonna do," he announced, rubbing his large rough hands together before the fire.

Bertha stirred in her chair and moaned slightly.

Howard looked her way. "You OK, Bertha?"

Her voice was plaintive. "I'm going to bed." She stood up uncertainly, pulled her shawl around her, and hobbled off to the back tent.

A long moment passed before Joy broke the silence. "How come Momma is sick all the time?"

Silence again.

Howard coughed, a deep cough from his chest. "Your momma's always been delicate, Joy Bell. But back around '36 she fell off a horse and got busted up bad. She never was the same after that." He stared at the floor, absorbed in some private, timeworn recollection. Then he looked up abruptly and focused his gaze on his children, determination animating his features. "But what we gotta decide now is . . . where do we go from here?"

They went to Sandy, Utah. Early in 1942, Howard Comstock moved his family to a rambling two-story house on Third East, the first of several dwellings they would occupy in the Salt Lake

area. Howard began working for Scribner's Trucking Company
out of Salt Lake City, delivering grocery supplies to stores
throughout Southern Utah and neighboring states. Often he was
gone from home for two or three months at a time. When he
returned, he would toss a roll of money in Bertha's lap and say,
"Will this hold you till next time?"

Although the house was a vast improvement over the tents,
life was no easier for Bertha, who found it increasingly difficult to
cope with the demands of her family. She was sick often, in bed
now most of the time. Her husband was constantly on the road,
and she never knew when Milt would take off for days at a time.
To make matters worse, her own dear mother died. As a
protective defense against multiple losses, Bertha became
oblivious to all that was happening around her.

No one in the family—not Bertha, nor Howard, nor any of the
children—seemed aware of the devastating factors already set in
motion to undermine the Comstock unity. Roy, not yet four,
would only vaguely recall the series of incidents which would
result in the ultimate disintegration of his family.

The first incident involved a tree house on the line between
the Comstock property and their neighbor's. The tree house
belonged to three youngsters who refused to grant the

Comstock children playing privileges in the coveted shelter. Bill and Richard figured they had as much right as anyone to play in it because it was half on their property. To make the situation more volatile, ornery neighbor boys would sit in their tree house and throw rocks at the Comstock back door to prevent the children from coming outdoors.

It didn't take Bill long to decide that he'd had enough of such treatment. One afternoon he took a can of gasoline, sneaked up into the tree house, and doused it thoroughly. As he shinnied down the tree, he tossed a lighted match through the window. The gasoline ignited instantly and flames engulfed the structure.

Spotting the fire, the enraged neighbor boys tumbled out of their house and sprinted across the yard, waving their arms like madmen. Bill ran for all he was worth, the shouting youngsters in close pursuit.

Breathless, he raced into the house and up the stairs to his mother's bedroom. The boys, screaming like banshees, followed close on his heels. Bill had only a moment to think before they would be upon him. His mother's room was empty. Then he remembered her kidney problem and the bedpan she kept under the bed. As the three youths dashed into the room, he heaved the contents of the pot into their surprised faces. Sputtering and furious, they lunged for him. He scurried under the bed. One boy swooped down and tugged on Bill's leg; another, on the opposite side, yanked one of his arms. Bill felt pulled in two.

The third boy set fire to the mattress. Soon smoke began to curl up out of the bedding. Then flames erupted. Coughing, the boys continued their tug-of-war. Bill's back scraped the bed springs as he strained his muscles to evade his captors.

Suddenly he heard sirens in the distance. Firemen were coming to quench the burning tree house. *And to put out the bed fire too,* he hoped desperately. His eyes and throat already stung. Soon all four boys gave in to fits of coughing. Still, none of them made an effort to leave the room.

The door opened. One boy stumbled out, hacking. The other two bolted down the stairs, choking. Bill scrambled out from under the blazing bed and bounded after them.

They met firemen coming up the stairs. And at the foot of the stairs stood police. Plus Drexel, their mother's friend, who was visiting today.

The four youths ground to a halt, dazed and gasping. Drexel, six feet tall, with menacing brows, grabbed Bill's arm and began shaking him. "What do you think you're doing, boy? Straighten up!"

His mother remained on the couch, too ill to respond. The twins sat on the floor, watching in wonder, their lower lips trembling. Without warning, Drexel wrenched Bill's arm and shoved him backward. When Bill careened against the wall the twins began to cry.

One policeman took hold of Drexel's arm and asked sharply, "Are you this boy's father?"

"Are you kidding?" Drexel retorted, shaking off the uniformed man's hold.

The officers had more questions. Who was the adult authority in the house? Why wasn't Bill in school?

"I don't have to go to school because Milt doesn't," Bill informed them.

"Who's Milt?" queried one policeman.

"Bill's older brother," replied Drexel. "When he's here he takes care of the house and kids."

"Where is this older boy?" inquired the other officer.

Bill shrugged. "I don't know. He hasn't been home in days."

Three days later Bill appeared in juvenile court. The judge lectured him, warning him not to set any more fires. But he added that he didn't feel the situation was entirely Bill's fault because, "obviously he doesn't have proper parental guidance." He told Bertha Comstock that if she didn't straighten things out in her household, she would lose her children.

A week and a half later, Howard Comstock returned to town. It was November of 1942—over a year since Johnnie's death. Howard rented a duplex on Eighth West and Prospect in Salt Lake City. Three days after he moved his family into their new home, he left town again.

The house on Prospect had a big black barn in back and a vacant lot next door. Milt and Bill took up smoking behind the barn, while Bill and Richard devised a money-making scheme using the vacant lot. The two boys dug themselves an underground hideout; then they stole items from a nearby five-and-ten-cent store and hid the merchandise in their secret chamber. Their scheme involved accomplices: the four-year-old twins. This would be Roy's first excursion into the world of crime—a twisted journey launched in childish innocence.

Roy wonders to this day whether the neighbors saw through the Comstock *modus operandi*. What did they think when little cherub-faced Roy showed up on their doorstep clutching a shiny kitchen utensil or a spool of thread and asked guilelessly, "Would you buy this for a dime? My momma needs some money"? Did they grow suspicious when the twins showed up time after time offering some brand-new garment or household item? If they did they never showed it. They always bought the merchandise.

An incident during the first week of December could easily have brought tragedy. It began harmlessly enough. Milt was home again. One afternoon he ambitiously baked twelve loaves of bread and proudly set them in a row on the kitchen table. They were beautiful, with gleaming, golden-brown crusts. And oh, the aroma!

Milt gathered the children around the table—Joy, Pansy, Richard, and the twins. He set out peanut butter, jelly, and butter for a royal feast. While he sliced bread and spread jelly for the youngsters, Bill came in carrying an old BB gun he had found somewhere in the backyard. Milt noticed that he had something else in his hand. A bullet.

"What's that?" asked Milt brusquely.

"This?" said Bill, holding up the shell. "Just an old bullet to a deer rifle."

Milt was irritated. "What'd you bring the gun in for?"

Bill stood at the head of the table looking down at the loaves of bread. "This gun won't hurt nobody. I took the insides out. See?" He held out the weapon. Then, on impulse he dropped the shell down the BB gun barrel and pulled the trigger. There was a sudden explosion and the barrel swelled like a watermelon. The bullet whizzed down the center of the table through twelve loaves of bread. It passed between Pansy and Richard's chairs, went through the table edge, through the wallboard, and out into the field. The youngsters jumped back frantically and stared in horror at a dumbfounded, ashen-faced Bill.

Milt was outraged. He was about to tear into Bill when he spied his mother in the doorway. She had been in the back bedroom sleeping, but now stood with her robe gathered around her. "What happened?" she mumured. "I heard a noise."

Milt nodded toward the gun. "It was just an accident."

"Went off by mistake," mumbled Bill.

"Well, be careful," she said, glassy-eyed. "Don't let anything like that happen again." Then she turned and went back to her room.

Bill sat down and fixed himself a sandwich. Milt, who had somehow managed to hold his temper to this point, picked up the butcher knife. It had jam on it. He recklessly wiped it on Bill's sleeve . . . and slit his brother's arm wide open. Both Milt and Bill stared in disbelief at the blood spurting from the gaping wound.

Milt sprang into action, grabbing tape, hurriedly making bandages and binding Bill's wound. He wrapped his own red handkerchief around the arm. The gash eventually healed, but none of the Comstock children would ever forget what happened that day with the bread, the BB gun, and the butcher knife.

Two weeks passed. It was the Christmas season. A light snowfall covered the ground. Streets and stores were decorated with bells, tinsel, and cardboard Santas. But Bill felt depressed. This year, too, the Comstocks would have no Christmas. Dad hadn't been home in weeks. Milt had taken off again, this time for good. There was hardly enough money for food.

Bill had watched the twins gaze longingly at the toys in the dime store window, but they were too little to know that Santa wouldn't come to their house. If only there was something he could do. *If only he could give the kids a nice Christmas!*

Bill was visiting a neighbor's house one afternoon when an idea occurred to him. He might be able to play Santa. A wallet lay on the dresser. For the moment there was no one around. He looked inside. Thirty-two dollars! He could take the money and who would know?

He hesitated only a second, then pocketed the cash. Within the hour he hitchhiked into Salt Lake City and enjoyed the shopping spree of his life. He bought a doll for each of the girls. Nice dolls with soft skin, and silky hair, and fancy dresses. And he purchased toy rifles and cowboy hats for Richard and the twins. He carried the presents home, walking on air. Never had he felt quite so giddy, so euphoric. He *was* Santa Claus! Because of him, the kids would have a Christmas.

As he approached his house he spotted a Christmas tree lying on someone's porch, waiting to be put up. Without thinking twice, he ran up, grabbed the tree, and took it with him. Somehow he made it home, his arms laden with parcels, dragging the tree behind him. Stealthily he hid his treasures in the barn.

On Christmas Eve, while the younger children slept, Bill carried the tree into the house and set it up. Carefully he placed the presents under it. It didn't matter that the tree was undecorated and the gifts unwrapped—they looked beautiful! Around daybreak Bill climbed up on the roof and stamped his feet; then he jumped down and rang the bell. After a moment he stole in the back door and made his way to the living room. There stood Roy and Ray staring wide-eyed at the tree. When they saw Bill, they bounced into his arms, both jabbering at once.

"Santa Claus came!" cried Roy. "I heard him on the roof and he rang the bell!"

"He brought us a tree and *toys!*" declared Ray, trying to outshout his brother.

Richard, Pansy, and Joy appeared, sleepy-eyed but awestruck by the apparent miracle of Christmas. Even Momma made it out of bed and joined the family around the tree as Bill handed out the presents. She didn't seem to think it strange that Santa Claus had come bearing gifts. Bill had feared that she might question him about this windfall, but she accepted the "miracle" as readily as did the children.

Pansy and Joy, their eyes glistening, hugged their dolls and rocked them tenderly in their arms. The twins and Richard put on their cowboy hats, aimed their rifles, and whooped and hollered, pretending to be Hopalong Cassidy or some other brave cowboy of the Old West.

When the gifts had been distributed, Pansy looked around with sudden concern and said, "Why is there no present for Bill?"

Everyone paused and looked curiously at Bill. Indeed, why *was* there no present for him?

Suddenly Roy jumped up and grabbed his older brother's leg in an affectionate bear hug. "Because he shot the rifle through the bread!" he exclaimed.

Everyone laughed. Of course. It was a perfectly logical explanation.

That afternoon Bill himself saw something of a miracle in the way his mother was responding to the celebration. She had come out of her self-imposed isolation and was actually enjoying the festivities. She even joined the children in singing Christmas carols: "Silent Night, Holy Night," "Away in a Manger," and "O Little Town of Bethlehem."

Then she took the family Bible, opened it, and read the Christmas story while the children listened, their faces luminous. It was a perfect day, the best Christmas Bill could remember. Never had there been such a spirit of joy and happiness in the Comstock home. In spite of Dad's and Milt's absence, they were truly a family after all!

Around five o'clock on Christmas day, there was an insistent knock on the door. Bill opened the door to two men.

"Detectives," they explained, flashing their badges.

"Are you Bill Comstock?" one man questioned.

Bill nodded.

"Then you'll have to come with us to the station."

Bill kept his gaze steady on the officers. "Right now?"

"I'm afraid so," said one. "You're under arrest. The charge is stealing."

"It took us a week to track you down," said the other man briskly. "What did you do with the money you stole from your neighbor?"

Bill gestured toward the gifts the children embraced. "There," he said.

The men hesitated a moment, exchanging uncertain glances. "I'm afraid we'll have to take those too," one said. The other nodded. Perfunctorily, they gathered up the toys.

In baffled silence, tears streaming down their faces, the girls relinquished their dolls. Richard ran into the other room with his hat and rifle. One of the officers brought him back. The twins stared in confusion at the stranger who held out his hand for the presents.

"Can't I keep my hat?" Roy asked softly.

The officer paused momentarily. His face reddened. "I'm sorry, son," he mumbled. Then, turning to Bill, he said, "Better get your coat, young man. It's cold outside."

Bertha sat speechless while Bill put on his overcoat and walked out the door with the two men. As quickly as they had come, the strangers were gone. They had taken Christmas with them.

But more than Christmas had been lost. Bill would not see his family again for nearly two and a half years. He would spend one year in reform school. Now only nine-year-old Pansy would be left to supervise the younger children. In a matter of months the entire Comstock family would be scattered. Roy Comstock would begin an odyssey that would carry him through fourteen foster homes in ten years' time and spawn emotional and spiritual traumas, leaving scars that would require still another decade to heal.

CHAPTER FIVE

As the summer of 1943 approached, Bertha Comstock's health worsened. Finally, when she required surgery and was admitted to the hospital, Howard Comstock returned home for a time and took a job driving a Sears truck. Meanwhile Pansy looked after Joy, Richard, and the twins.

The warm, sticky days of June and July dragged on. Bertha failed to improve. Howard stopped at the hospital each evening after work to spend some time with his wife. But on arriving home after ten each night, his face drawn with discouragement, he had to tell Pansy, "Sorry, baby, no change."

One morning Pansy turned to her brothers and sister and said, "Momma's still too sick to come home." The children were disappointed. They had hoped their mother would be home in time for Richard's birthday. Joy had even circled July 28 on the calendar. Now the day had arrived and the children had nothing to give him, no way to celebrate. Pansy and Joy scoured the house and found colored paper and birthday candles. They decided to make Richard some candle holders.

"What can I do with these?" he wanted to know.

Pansy thought a moment. An idea struck. "You know those old bedbugs that are always biting us? Well, I heard the way to get rid of them is to burn them out of the mattress."

Richard grinned mischievously. "I hate them dumb old bugs. Let's go burn 'em!"

"Yeah!" chorused the twins.

Nothing had caused such excitement in the Comstock household for weeks. The youngsters scurried pell-mell upstairs and raced one another for the bed. There they gathered around and watched in rapt attention as Richard lighted a candle and poised the flame over the offensive mattress.

"How do we know if we got 'em?" asked Joy. No one seemed to know.

A black spot spread where the flame touched fiber. The children took turns chasing the elusive lice with their devastating magic flame. Black spots appeared like polka dots.

"This is no fun," Richard said at last. "We'd have to burn up the whole bed to be sure we killed all the bugs."

"Yeah," Joy agreed. "Let's go feed the chickens."

Nearly five hundred yellow baby chicks skittered about in the chicken coop behind the house. Only Pansy could enter the coop to feed the chickens. Daddy had said so. The other youngsters could fill water dishes and hand them to her through the window.

They were tossing feed into the coop when they heard two neighbor boys scream. "Hey, your house is on fire!"

Smoke billowed from the upstairs bedroom window.

"Oh, no, the mattress!" gasped Pansy.

The neighbor youths dashed into the house and, minutes later, pushed a smoldering mattress out the window. The Comstock children watched dumbfounded. Pansy could only think, *What will Daddy say?*

That night when Howard came in late, he found his brood huddled together on the living room floor, asleep. He knelt down and shook Pansy. "What happened? Why are you all down here?"

Pansy sat up and rubbed her eyes. "We were afraid to go upstairs."

"Why?"

"We—we tried to burn the bedbugs out of the mattress."

Howard expelled a sharp breath. "So that's what I smelled!"

Pansy began to weep. "I'm sorry, Daddy."

He tousled her hair. "Don't cry, baby. It's OK. Go back to sleep."

Howard was reluctant to go to work the next morning, but he

had no choice. "Just don't let anything happen today," he warned Pansy.

She promised. But the situation was already beyond her control. Around noon a pleasant-faced, nicely dressed woman arrived. "I'm from the Child Welfare Department," she told Pansy sweetly. "Your neighbor called me about the fire yesterday—and about you children being alone. She thought you might need help."

Pansy eyed her suspiciously. "No, ma'am, we don't need no help."

"I think perhaps you do. May I come inside?"

The woman didn't stay long. She looked around, checked the kitchen cupboards, asked a few questions, then said, "Where's the telephone?"

"Don't have none," said Joy.

The woman looked from Pansy to Joy. "I'm going next door to make a phone call. Then I'll be back for you children."

"Are you going to take us away?" asked Pansy warily.

The woman's smile froze momentarily. Gently she said, "We'll talk about that when I come back, honey."

When the woman had gone, Pansy tremblingly gathered Joy, Richard, and the twins around her. She felt scared inside. She wanted to run. She wanted to take the youngsters and hide somewhere until Daddy came home. But where could she hide four little kids until ten o'clock at night? And what would they do for food?

After a moment the trembling subsided and Pansy could think more clearly. Perhaps there was no way out of this, but she would be prepared. She steered the reluctant twins into the bathroom and washed their faces. She made Richard scrub his arms and knees. She helped Joy change into a clean dress.

Then she slipped into her parents' room. It was silent, as hushed as a grave. She could hear her own breathing. If only Daddy were here. If only Momma weren't sick in the hospital! Oh, why didn't Momma hurry up and get well?

Pansy opened her mother's bureau drawer and removed one of her best handkerchiefs. She pressed it against her cheek. It felt like silk, like Momma's soft skin. She tucked it into the front of her dress. One of her mother's prettiest pins lay on the dresser among several other pieces of costume jewelry. Pansy picked it up and pinned it to her dress. She studied her image in the mirror. Yes, she was as ready now as she could be.

That afternoon, July 29, the woman from the Welfare Department drove the Comstock children to the county hospital where doctors examined them for illness or sores. Pansy was sitting on a bench in the hall waiting her turn when she spied her father coming up the front steps. She ran to meet him.

"Daddy! I knew you'd come!"

They embraced briefly, then he held her at arm's length. "Pansy, what are you doing here?"

Now it was Pansy's turn to look puzzled. "Didn't you come to take us home, Daddy?"

He shook his head blankly. "I came to visit your momma."

Pansy clasped his hand tightly as the welfare lady approached.

"Mr. Comstock?" the woman asked.

"Yeah, that's me. What's goin' on here?"

"I need to talk with you—privately."

Her father went off to one side and talked with the woman for what seemed a very long time. Finally he came back and sat down beside Pansy. In his face she saw lines that she hadn't noticed before. He cleared his throat, but his voice still sounded gravelly.

"Pansy, baby, me and the lady talked it over, and we figure it's best for you kids to stay somewhere else for a while until Momma can take care of you again."

"Where?"

He avoided her eyes. His words sounded splintered. "A . . . foster home."

The months that followed were topsy-turvy for the entire Comstock clan. For a few weeks the children stayed with a man named Hans, who made Sears deliveries with Howard Comstock. But when Bertha was still not able to be released from the hospital, the children were split up. Pansy and Joy went to one home, Roy and Ray to another, and Richard to still another.

Thirteen different foster homes in five years' time. That's what Roy Comstock would remember in years to come. The names, the faces, the houses would remain blurred in his memory. For a time he and Ray were placed with Pansy and Joy. Another time the twins were separated from their sisters. And eventually Roy and Ray were sent to separate homes.

Shortly after the children had been parceled out to foster homes, Howard and Bertha Comstock were divorced. Howard met and married a woman named Susan, and from time to time the two attempted to make a home for the Comstock children in Knab, Utah. But his attempts to reunite the family were unsuccessful.

Bertha Comstock also tried briefly to provide a home for her children once more, but her effort proved as fruitless as Howard's. Living on welfare in a shabby hotel room, she had little to offer the youngsters. Still, she delighted in taking them with her to the neighborhood bar or pool hall to meet her friends or to watch a game of shuffleboard.

Ultimately both Bertha and Howard accepted the fact that they could not keep their children. The break had to be final, permanent. Although Bertha would continue to visit her children from time to time in the years to come, Howard severed all ties with his offspring and would not see them again for nearly ten years.

In the beginning, four-year-old Roy was too young to comprehend what was happening to him. Shuttled from home to home, staying with strangers, then with Momma or Daddy, packing and unpacking his meager parcel of clothes, always saying hello or goodbye was a normal way of life for Roy. In the first few homes, he still had Ray for security when he felt sad or lonely. It was almost as good as being with Momma and Daddy.

But not all of the homes offered love and security. In one home, a farm, Roy and Ray were forced to carry a heavy chain out to the field and back each day—a chain used to rig the tractor to the plow. The farmer, a huge, gruff, unfeeling man, was severe in meting out punishment for supposed misdeeds. Roy, who had a bed-wetting problem, learned this sober fact all too soon. Waking that first morning to a wet bed and scarcely having cleared his mind of sleep, Roy felt himself being uprooted and shoved outside the old frame house, where the farmer rubbed his bare bottom in the snow.

"This'll teach you!" the angry man boomed.

After that, each time Roy wet the bed the farmer dragged him outside and, in spite of Roy's screams, forced him to experience that excruciating humiliation. Roy grew increasingly afraid to go to sleep at night, afraid he would fall asleep and wet the bed, afraid the man would take him out into the snow. He fought off sleep until his body ached with weariness. Couldn't give in to it . . . couldn't give in . . . couldn't—Then suddenly he would awake and realize in dismay that it was morning. Inevitably his sheet was soaked. Even before the man came in, Roy could feel the ice-fire sting of cold snow on his bare bottom.

In years to come Roy would remember most of his foster homes more by his fears and the fantasies than by the people who cared for him. At one home it was necessary to make nocturnal trips to the outhouse. Whenever Roy undertook this perilous journey, the other youngsters in the home thrived on taunting him with "The boogyman will get you!" Roy had no choice but to summon his courage and trek out into the darkness anyway. But one night as he crept cautiously along, the echo of "boogyman" playing in his ears, a rooster suddenly jumped on his shoulder. Convinced that he was being attacked by the imaginary creature, Roy tore back into the house in stark terror, wetting his pants en route.

When Roy was nearly seven years old, he and Ray went to live with a Mormon family just outside Salt Lake City. Mr. Merrill was a kind man who dug a large hole in the vacant lot next door and put beams across it to make a play hideout for the boys. Devoutly religious, the Merrills instructed the boys in Mormonism. In 1947, when Roy and Ray were eight years old, they were baptized as Mormons in the tabernacle at Salt Lake City.

A vivid memory Roy would carry with him from those early years was of a devastating flood. Roy was in an upstairs bedroom looking out the window when he spied a fierce wall of water inundating the street and rushing toward the house. The water violently swept away automobiles as though they were plastic toys. The house shook. The noise was deafening. The water rushed by the front door and uprooted the fence, but the house remained intact. Roy stood spellbound.

That experience deepened Roy's fears and anxieties. Along with his apprehensions, his dreams and fantasies now occurred more frequently. His sleep was often marred by bizarre nightmares. He woke up screaming night after night, convinced a witch was going to kill him. He also dreamed the school bus was coming to take him to school, but somehow he missed the bus, so he had to walk the two miles alone. He would wake up with his heart pounding, haunted by the recurring fear that he would get lost and no one would ever find him.

While with the Merrills, Roy completed the second grade, only to learn that he was being held back a year. It was a disappointment, not being promoted to third grade with the rest of his class. But it was no wonder he had problems with school. In moving from place to place, he had missed kindergarten entirely; and how often had he changed schools during first grade? He couldn't remember. Besides, he had more on his mind than reading, writing, and arithmetic.

To combat his fears and anxieties he became adept at making up stories. He imagined himself fighting lions and ripping bears into pieces. He pictured himself a hero. What's more, he shared his fantasies with his classmates. In spite of their scoffing he would insist, "I killed a lion with my bare hands. On my way to school today. Really." The stories eased Roy's loneliness and lessened his sense of helplessness. As long as he had his fantasies he would survive.

Often Roy's fantasies involved his father. He could hardly remember his dad now, but he treasured what memories he had. He recalled his father's big strong body; he was a giant with huge shoulders and hands like iron. Roy told his classmates that his father was off fighting a war. "If he wasn't fighting he'd be here and you'd see how big he is," Roy would assert. "My dad's a real giant."

At night Roy would lie awake and pull bit and pieces of memory from the past—his father, his father's voice, his constant cough. What did his father look like? A tanned rough-skinned man in bib overalls, a big heavy jacket, large boots, and a cowboy hat. But Roy couldn't remember his face, couldn't visualize his features. What was wrong that his dad's face remained a blank?

Roy thought, too, of his mother—a pale, soft-spoken woman wrapped in a shawl, rocking gently, or lying in bed reading magazines. She never got angry. But Roy couldn't remember her ever saying much either.

The fantasies and memories didn't always work for Roy. When

the pain broke through he felt defenseless against the knowledge that nobody really cared about him; no one loved him. Then the questions stung like barbs: *Why me? How come my parents don't love me? Why can't I have a mom and dad like other kids?*

CHAPTER SIX

It's a bird . . . it's a plane . . . it's Superman!
Superman.
Roy's fantasies had found a focal point. Personification. The comic book character had become Roy's hero. He was obsessed by the idea of meeting Superman—and yes, of actually *becoming* the brave, daring man of steel. It was possible. It had to be.

Roy had found a friend in another foster child staying with the Merrills—a boy named Gary who shared Roy's vision of becoming the super hero. The two spent hours together playing, pretending, and devouring Superman comic books.

One afternoon as they walked home from school, Gary remarked, "When my mom comes to see me again, she's gonna buy me a Superman tee shirt."

Roy tried not to sound impressed. "So?"

"So that's almost as good as having a Superman suit."

"Is not."

"Is too. Bet your mom wouldn't buy you one."

"She would if she was here," countered Roy.

"Fat chance of that. She never comes around."

"She did once," said Roy. "She took me for a ride."

"You mean when she showed up with that guy in his noisy jalopy?"

Roy kicked a stone and watched it skitter up the road like something alive. "Yeah, that was the time," he mumbled.

Gary swung his foot and sent the stone another twenty feet. "Didn't you say your mom almost got killed that day?"

Roy ground his jaw slightly. It wasn't a pleasant memory. Speedy Jack, Momma's boyfriend, had driven around town with a bottle of beer in his hand, guzzling whenever he pleased. Once when he shot wildly around a corner, tires squealing, the door flew open and Momma almost fell out of the car. Roy couldn't wait to get back to the Merrills after that. But he hadn't seen his mother since then.

"That was a long time ago," he told Gary vaguely, avoiding his friend's eyes. "I don't remember much what happened."

"How come your mom don't come around anymore?" Gary wanted to know.

Roy swallowed hard. "She's awful busy. But she'd be here every day if she could." He wondered if he sounded convincing.

They were almost home now. Gary stopped, picked up a stick, and sent it spinning through the air. He looked at Roy.

Accepting the challenge, Roy grabbed a twig and pitched it skyward. "Beat you by a mile," he gloated.

Gary was skeptical. "Well, if I had me a Superman suit—"

Roy shot back with, "Well, you don't, and you won't ever!"

A conspiratorial gleam lighted Gary's eyes. He nudged Roy's arm. "What if I told you we could get Superman suits and be just like Superman?"

Roy frowned. "How?"

Gary's words came faster. "And what would you say if we could *meet* Superman?"

Roy's pulse quickened. Meet Superman? The idea set fire to his imagination. It was his choicest dream, for in his mind lurked the suspicion that Superman was really his father in disguise. But he dared not share this notion even with Gary.

"How could we meet Superman?" Roy asked.

Gary pointed a finger toward the horizon. "See that mountain? I heard of this place just over that mountain where there's this big ranch. If we go there, we can get Superman suits and fly right out of the world. We'll be just like Superman!"

Roy kicked distractedly at the pavement. "You really think so?"

"Sure," said Gary breathlessly. "I'll go if you go."

Roy shook his head. "It would look like we was running away from home. I don't want the Merrills to think we don't like 'em."

Grudgingly Gary muttered, "Well, if you change your mind . . . ."

Roy did change his mind—for a totally unexpected reason. The events of one afternoon altered his life profoundly. Roy was on his way to the grocery store to run an errand for Mrs. Merrill. He had money jingling in his pocket along with a list of items to purchase. He was strutting along the sidewalk when he spotted her—his mother—walking toward him with a strange man on each arm. Roy's first impulse was to call out, "Hi, Momma!" But the words died in his throat. The sight of those men's faces turned his elation into deep disappointment. His mother didn't even notice him! The three approached, arms interlocked, swaying together, his mother laughing, twittering nonsense, the men guffawing.

Roy's heart pounded savagely. He wanted to turn and run, but his limbs refused to move. Then, incredibly, his mother and the rowdy-looking strangers turned and went into a bar. Gone, just like that!

Roy remained motionless, the taste of anger in his mouth. For one blind instant he wished he had thrown something at his mother—to get her attention, to make her notice him, to make her hurt like he hurt now. *I was standing right here and she didn't even see me*, he marveled.

He forced himself to move. His steps felt awkward, sluggish. It was as if he had been struck hard, as if his mind and body were struggling to recover from a terrible blow. The pain was intolerable. He trudged toward home, his head down. A lump the size of a doorknob swelled in his throat. Unspilled tears blurred his vision. He wanted to cry. But no, he wouldn't. Couldn't!

He found a narrow alley between two buildings not far from the Merrills' house. Privacy! He crouched down beside a stack of old crates and pressed his face against the rough splintery surface of the wood. He cried bitterly, his chest heaving, until the sobs came out choked and dry. Then he sat up and wiped his eyes with the back of his hands, vowing that he would never let anyone make him cry again. A shell of anger and resentment began coating the pain.

He stood up, smoothed his jeans, and tucked in his shirt. His jaw hardened. He wasn't quite nine yet, but in the last few minutes he had aged several years. He saw things clearly now. His mother had deserted her children, leaving them in the care of strangers, so that she could go out and have a good time and do as she pleased. It was enough to fill a guy with hate! But even Roy didn't realize that the seed of bitterness which had just taken root would be his principal motivation for the next ten years.

Now more than ever Roy wanted to become the legendary man of steel. Then he wouldn't let anything—or anyone—ever touch him again. The next day he told Gary he was ready to trek over the mountain in search of Superman. Gary was too charged with excitement to notice Roy's dark mood. Stuffing his clothes—tee shirts, socks and jeans—into a paper bag, Gary said, "D'ya think Ray would wanta go with us?"

Roy brightened momentarily. If only Ray would go with them! Roy dreaded leaving his twin behind. Ray was all the family he had now. The two of them had grown to depend on each other for so much—Roy helping Ray with his schoolwork, Ray taking Roy's side against neighborhood bullies. But would Ray go with them in search of Superman? "Naw, he wouldn't wanta go," Roy replied. "He thinks we're stupid for believing in Superman."

"Aw, Ray's always the goody-goody anyway," growled Gary, punching some underwear into the sack. "But we'll show 'im."

"What we gonna do for money?"

Gary nodded toward a closed door across the hall. "I seen some cash on the dresser in there."

Roy followed his buddy's gaze. Gary meant the bedroom of the Merrills' oldest son.

"*Steal* from him?"

"Why not? We need cash. He must have five bucks sittin' there for all the world to see. And he already left for school, so who's to know?"

Moments later the boys were scooping nickels, dimes, and half dollars off the bureau into their pockets when they heard someone shuffle into the room. *Caught!* They wheeled around, Roy guiltily stuffing his fists into his pockets, Gary knocking the remaining change to the floor. "Ray!" stammered Roy.

Ray looked blankly from one boy to the other. "What are you guys doing with that money?"

"We're gonna run away and find Superman," Gary announced, jutting out his chin defiantly.

"We need the money," explained Roy.

"That Superman stuff is crazy," argued Ray. "You'll just get into trouble."

Roy went over and put a comradely arm around his brother. "Come with us, Ray. It won't be no fun without you."

Ray looked away. "I can't. It's not right. The Merrills would be mad."

Roy tightened his grip on Ray's shoulder. "Are you gonna snitch on us?"

Ray looked at his twin, anguish twisting his expression. "You shouldn't take that money—"

"I gotta know, Ray. Are you gonna tell?"

Ray bit hard on his lower lip. "Naw, I won't tell."

For a moment the brothers embraced awkwardly, and in that instant Roy wished he had never agreed to go looking for Superman. But he had to go. And Ray must never know his reason—the bitter truth about their mother.

Roy and Gary left that morning, skipping school and thumbing a ride to the base of the mountain. After buying apples and candy bars at a little grocery they hiked up into the foothills until their muscles ached and their feet were blistered. That evening, sore and hungry, they collapsed in exhaustion on the bare wood floor of an old abandoned shack and slept until morning. Then they set out again, climbing over rocks, trudging through thick weeds, following winding, rutted roads.

"It can't be far now," wheezed Gary as they pushed through a patch of stubborn thicket.

Catching a second wind, Roy sprinted ahead of his buddy. He scaled one rocky knoll, then another. He felt a sweet breathless exhilaration. Almost there. They had to be!

Suddenly Roy's foot struck a rock with painful force. Tripping, he plummeted downhill and rolled helplessly over loose stones and spiky brush. At the foot of a steep incline he found himself sprawled on the ground, dazed and bleeding.

Gary scrambled after him and knelt down on one knee. "You OK?"

"Yeah, sure."

"Comstock, I can't believe you did that."

"Me either." Roy turned his head aside and spit out blood. Gary craned his neck closer. "Man, you knocked out your front tooth!"

Roy stuck his tongue in the tiny cavity, then spit again. "Yeah, I sure did." Gingerly he stretched out his legs and tried to move his torso. He groaned. "I think I broke my arm too."

"It sure don't look good," observed Gary weakly.

Roy unbuttoned his shirt. Gary helped him out of it, then wrapped the garment around the oozing gash. Roy stumbled to his feet. He and Gary plodded toward the road, heads down, silent. Roy's arm throbbed, but his disappointment hurt worse than the broken arm.

"It was a wild-goose chase," he mumbled, giving Gary a sidelong glance. "We're not gonna find Superman, not ever in our whole lives."

Gary stared sullenly down the narrow mountain road. He didn't answer.

After a while an automobile pulled to a stop beside them—an old model with a noisy, coughing engine. "Looks like you boys could use a lift to the hospital," the driver said, leaning across to open the door.

The boys spent the rest of the day in a nearby hospital emergency room. That evening the police escorted them home. The Merrills, relieved to learn that their foster children had been found relatively unharmed, welcomed them back with open arms. But the welfare authorities were less charitable. Declaring Roy "incorrigible" for stealing and running away, they separated him from his brother Ray and shipped him to still another foster home, to another family of strangers.

CHAPTER SEVEN

Although Roy grieved over his separation from Ray, he nevertheless found the stability he needed with Robert and Verna Shelton. On December 1, 1948, he moved into the Shelton house at 4400 South 9th East in Salt Lake City. This would be his home for the next five years. Here he would experience his first real sense of normalcy, and establish standards and values which would be important to him in years to come.

The Sheltons were a comfortable upper-middle-class family with a large house on an acre of land. Strict Seventh-Day Adventists with a strong sense of family and a love for children, Bob and Verna had five youngsters of their own—three daughters and two sons. They also kept a steady stream of foster children coming and going through their home— sometimes as many as fifteen youngsters at once.

Uncle Bob and Aunt Verna—as the Sheltons were affectionately tagged by their foster children—treated each child like a member of the family. Boys and girls from reform school or broken homes received the same love, respect, and discipline as their own children.

The Shelton house was roomy and pleasant. While the foster boys shared a large bedroom with six bunk beds, the foster girls occupied an enclosed back porch with a clear view of a winding, rippling creek. Across the creek was another acre of land on which Bob Shelton had built a small house where he often made candy for the children to sell. When the weather was warm they went swimming in the creek, or fishing, or sailing on the big raft that Uncle Bob had built. Or they ran along the water's edge catching frogs and snakes.

Verna Shelton was a short stocky woman who ran the house on a tight schedule, disciplined the children with a firm hand, and allowed no child to enter the house without first removing his shoes. Roy learned quickly how to perform daily household tasks—scrubbing floors, polishing furniture, emptying trash, washing dishes, ironing clothes. (Even blue jeans had to be pressed!)

But what Roy would remember most about Aunt Verna was not her immaculate house but her extraordinary sense of fairness. One incident especially left an indelible impression. One summer day Jerry, the Sheltons' youngest son, unexpectedly discovered Roy and one of the foster girls out in the field kissing.

"I'm telling Mom!" Jerry cried, sprinting toward the house.

Roy bounded after him, shouting, "Come on, don't tell. What's the big deal? I was just learning a few facts of life."

"When Mom hears this she'll teach you plenty," replied Jerry breathlessly. "You won't sit down for a year!"

Jerry delivered his report and Mrs. Shelton confronted Roy with the accusation. Roy denied it. There was a stalemate as each boy insisted he was telling the truth. The tension grew as the boys awaited Verna Shelton's decision. Finally she said, "All right, Roy, I believe you. Go play." Turning to her son, she warned, "Jerry, I don't want you telling tales to get Roy into trouble. Behave yourself, you hear?"

Roy gloated over winning that round with Jerry, but he felt something else too—a prick of guilt for deceiving Aunt Verna and a growing admiration for this woman who would actually take his side against her own child.

As Roy's affection for Aunt Verna grew, so did his respect for Uncle Bob. Bob Shelton was a tall thin man with dark hair and a fair complexion. For a time he worked as a book salesman and traveled frequently. Later he took a job as an orderly in a hospital and remained there until he retired. In summer he bravely carted his sizable family on annual vacation trips. One year eleven of them traveled in Uncle Bob's nine-passenger

DeSoto Suburban automobile. In the summer of 1951 the family drove to Missouri and bought an old milk truck, which, after coming home, they used for peddling candy.

Bob Shelton saw to it that each family member was in church every Saturday. Roy, who attended church only because he had to, was skeptical about God. If God really cared about him, why did he let his family break up? Roy was convinced that religion really didn't work anyway. Over the years he had been in and out of so many homes. Each home had its own set of rules, its own idea of who God was and how to reach heaven. Roy tried not to think much about God. He figured religion was for old women and little kids, not for him.

Roy's move to the Shelton home resulted in a permanent separation between Roy and his twin brother Ray. The social services authorities made it clear that under no circumstances were the twins to be in touch with each other. "You were becoming too dependent on your brother," Roy was told. Years later Roy learned that Ray, who was living with the Nelson family in Salt Lake City, was given the same excuse: he had grown too dependent on Roy.

The authorities may have been trying to prepare the twins for adoption by different families. Several times the Sheltons discussed the possibility of adopting Roy, for while other foster children came and went, Roy remained, becoming more and more a part of the family. Roy himself enjoyed living with the Sheltons; he knew what to expect from them. The only thing troubling him was the fact that if the Sheltons adopted him he wouldn't be a Comstock anymore.

But as much as Roy wanted to remain a Comstock, he wanted nothing more to do with his mother. His resentment toward her had swelled beyond all rational proportions. He hated her. He was convinced it was her fault the family had fallen apart. And always, always in his memory was the odious picture of his mother, laughing and drunk, reeling into the bar with two strange men.

From time to time Bertha Comstock came to visit Roy at the Shelton home. Invariably Roy ran and hid in the crawl space under the house, refusing to see his mother. When she sent presents for his birthday or Christmas, he took the gifts into the backyard, gathered the other children around, and set fire to the packages. As the fancy paper and ribbons were consumed in flames, Roy stared in mute fascination, thinking darkly, *This is how much I hate you, Momma. This is how much I hate you!*

While Roy dreaded his mother's visits, he looked forward to seeing his oldest brother. Twenty-year-old Milt was making the Navy his career. On Milt's first visit Roy didn't recognize the grinning, curly headed sailor who stood before him.

"Man, have you ever grown!" Milt exclaimed, opening his arms. "Look at you. You're gonna be taller than me!"

Roy allowed himself to be embraced. He felt awkward, having so few memories of his big brother.

To give themselves a chance to get reacquainted, Milt suggested a walk, a little chat. Milt did most of the talking. "I saw your brother Bill the other day. He's in the Army now. Doing real good."

"Good," mumbled Roy. He couldn't quite remember what Bill looked like.

"He's an amateur boxer," Milt continued. "Even fought the Golden Gloves in Madison Square Garden in New York. Bet you didn't know that."

Roy shook his head. "Did you see him fight?"

"Naw. Wish I had, though. He's a big man, your brother. Not even twenty years old, and already over six feet five."

Roy whistled. "Boy, I'd sure like to see him."

Milt grinned. "You will. He's coming to see you real soon."

They shuffled on amiably, their arms casually brushing together as they walked. Roy felt good being with Milt again. After all these years the bond between them was still there. If there was anybody he could count on, it was Milt.

Milt broke into Roy's thoughts with: "I checked on your brother Richard. He's not having an easy time of it. Welfare can't find a foster home for him. He's a bit slow, too, so school's hard for him."

"That's too bad," said Roy, but he really didn't want to talk about Richard now. He looked admiringly at Milt. "Your uniform is really neat. What do you do in the Navy?"

Milt chuckled and playfully mussed Roy's hair. "Lots, boy. More'n you'd believe. I joined the Navy when I was seventeen. Got Mom to sign for me. It's been good for me too." His voice grew serious. "But I can't tell you the times I've spent on that ship staring out at the sea thinking about you kids. Sometimes I'd almost go crazy wondering where you and Ray and Joy were—and if you were OK."

"We were OK, Milt," Roy assured him.

Milt looked away, his voice low and quavering. "I'd think about Johnnie too, and feel so lousy inside, lousy for the whole mess our family got into. I keep thinking I shoulda done something. I don't know, maybe it was my fault—"

They walked on in uneasy silence for several minutes. Roy considered telling Milt that their mother was the one responsible for all their troubles, but he had the feeling he'd only get an argument.

After a while Milt reached over and squeezed Roy's shoulder. "How about Ray?" he asked. "Do you ever see Ray?"

Roy shook his head. "Never. I don't know where he went. I don't guess I'll ever see him again." Roy scuffed his shoe along the sidewalk. Thinking of Ray made him feel as if he had lost something important. He felt sad inside, but he pushed the thought away.

Milt spoke again, sounding cheerful. "So how's life with the Sheltons?"

"We do lots of stuff," replied Roy. "Uncle Bob lets us make candy and raise banty roosters and swim in the creek. I swim real good."

"Sounds great," said Milt approvingly. "The Sheltons seem like real nice folks. And they sure got a pretty daughter."

Roy looked up and frowned. "You mean Nina?"

"Yeah. Nina. I wouldn't mind getting to know her better."

"She's OK . . . for a *girl*."

When the brothers returned from their walk, Milt made it a point to visit with attractive Nina Shelton. This was the beginning of a serious relationship. Eventually he and Nina would be married, Milt becoming Bob and Verna Shelton's son-in-law.

In the summer of 1952 Roy spent a lot of time at a nearby high school pool. One afternoon after an hour in the water, he hoisted himself up on the side of the pool to catch his breath. Glancing across the pool he saw something that made him do a doubletake. Not something—*someone!* His brother Ray!

Or was he mistaken? Could it really be Ray? Roy squinted

hard. He couldn't be sure. He hadn't seen Ray in years. He dived in and swam to the opposite side where the boy stood. Bursting up out of the water, he shouted, "Ray?"

The boy turned around. Recognition spread across his face. "Roy!"

Roy clambered out of the pool. Whooping and laughing, the brothers hugged each other joyously. "Man, where have you been?" cried Roy.

"Not far from here," said Ray.

"Same here," panted Roy, mopping his wet blond hair out of his eyes. "Let's go somewhere and talk."

Ray glanced around and laughed sheepishly. "Yeah. The guys must think we're crazy standing here hugging each other."

"I don't care what they think!" said Roy.

They raced arm in arm to the locker room, dressed, then walked together to the Shelton house.

"You sure got tall," said Ray.

"You sure didn't," mused Roy. "I guess we don't look like twins anymore."

"Guess not."

"Where do you live?" asked Roy.

"Near Granite High School."

Roy shook his head in disbelief. "So close? And all this time we never ran into each other!"

"Where do you go to school?"quizzed Ray.

"I just graduated from Lincoln Elementary. I start junior high this fall."

"Do you like your foster folks?"

Roy nodded. "The Sheltons are OK, but they've got fifteen kids in the house, counting their own. So sometimes it's a mad scramble for the bathroom."

"Man, I guess so!"

"Meals are the worst," remarked Roy solemnly. "We don't eat meat."

"You're kidding!"

"Nope. Aunt Verna even makes meat loaf out of soybeans."

Ray wrinkled his nose. "How do you stand it?"

Roy shrugged. "For a while I was hungry all the time, especially for meat. But things are better now."

"Better? How?"

"Aunt Verna gave me garbage detail."

"So what?"

Roy grinned knowingly. "So I gobble up all the leftovers and there's nothing left to throw in the trash." He paused for a breath, then said, "So what's your home like?"

"It's really neat," Ray told him eagerly. "I live on a horse ranch. Got my own colt. We go to rodeos all the time and break in horses. I'm the Nelsons' only foster child, so they treat me like their own kid."

Roy whistled. "Their only kid!"

"What do you do at your place?"

Roy hesitated, then replied dryly, "I wash dishes, iron clothes, and, like I said, take out the garbage."

Ray looked dubious. "You must do more than that."

"Yeah! I sell candy and take violin lessons. This summer I got a job picking tomatoes and feeding the mink on our neighbor's ranch."

"Oh, well, that sounds like . . . fun." Ray's voice trailed off.

Roy nudged his brother good-naturedly. "Come on, man. You never could lie!"

They both laughed.

Arriving home, Roy proudly introduced his twin to the Shelton household. It was an unforgettable day for the boys, finding each other again.

But their joy was short-lived. When Ray returned home and related his good news, he was grounded for going to the Sheltons and coming home late without permission. Once again the welfare department stepped in. Without offering an explanation, they made it clear that the boys were not to see each other again. From time to time the twins met briefly, surreptitiously, but always over their meetings loomed the unspoken fear that they would be caught and punished.

CHAPTER EIGHT

One afternoon in the spring of 1953 there was an insistent knock on the Shelton door. Roy answered it, opening the door to two men. One was his Uncle Carl, who visited occasionally. The other was a stranger—a tall man with immense shoulders and a tan, leathery face.

"Hello, Roy," said Uncle Carl, his voice a bit loud and somehow forced. Roy noticed that his face looked curiously strained, intense. The men came inside and stood in awkward silence for a moment. Roy glanced around for Aunt Verna. He really didn't want visitors today, not when he was planning a secret meeting with Ray.

Uncle Carl gestured toward the man beside him. "Roy, do you know who this is?"

Roy gazed without interest at the stranger. "No."

"This is your father."

Roy met the man's gaze. "Hi," he mumbled.

Uncle Carl gripped Roy's shoulder affectionately, a brisk, persuasive gesture. His voice was still too loud, edged with a brittle cheerfulness. "How about this boy, Howard? All grown up, huh? Just turned fourteen, didn't you, Roy?"

Roy nodded, staring at the floor. He felt his father's eyes piercing him.

"How long has it been since you two saw each other?" Uncle Carl pressed on. "Ten years? That long?"

"Something like that," replied Howard Comstock.

Roy eased out of Uncle Carl's grip. "I got things to do," he said.

"But your dad came all the way from California to see you," Uncle Carl told him firmly.

"I'll get Aunt Verna," said Roy. He called his foster mother but didn't wait for the round of introductions. Escaping to his room, he sat on his bed and marveled over what had just happened. His father had stood in the same room with him and it didn't matter. He felt nothing! It struck him suddenly that after having fourteen fathers over the past ten years, one more didn't make much difference.

Moments later, Roy stole quietly out the back door for his meeting with Ray. The two walked to a local grocery where they bought ice-cold bottles of root beer. Waiting for his change, Roy told his twin about his surprise visitor. "Just think," he said, "Dad was standing right there and all I could think was, 'Big deal!' "

"That's how I felt when he came to see me," said Ray, snapping the cap off his pop bottle.

"What is he doing here, anyway?"

"Uncle Carl says Mom and Dad might get married again. He says Dad wants to get us kids together and take us to California."

"What for?"

"Maybe he figures we're old enough to work for him. Uncle Carl says he has his own business now."

Roy smashed his fist against the counter. "Why don't they just leave me alone? Aunt Verna and Uncle Bob are my family now!"

The grocer, returning with Roy's change, gave him a quizzical look. "You OK, buddy?"

"Yeah, sure!" Roy scooped up the coins and stuffed them in his pocket. To Ray he added, "I don't know if we'll ever be OK."

One day that June, as Roy picked tomatoes in a neighbor's field, he heard the sputter of an engine on the road behind him. He plucked another large tomato and placed it in the box, then turned around and squinted toward the road. Someone in the bed of the truck was waving.

Roy wiped the sweat off his forehead and trudged toward the pickup. As he approached he spotted his mother and father in the cab—and his brothers and sisters in the back. He stopped short. He wasn't about to confront his mother. He turned away, feeling that familiar knot of anger in the pit of his stomach.

"Roy, wait!" The voice was Pansy's. She climbed out of the truck and padded toward him. Stopping a few feet away she shielded her eyes from the blistering sun. "Roy, don't you want to talk a minute?"

He eyed her skeptically. "About what?"

"Us. The family. Mom and Dad are getting back together. They want all you kids with them."

"*All* of us? Milt can't go. He's in the Navy."

"No, but Bill's coming. He just got out of the Army."

"Are you going?"

"Well, no, not me either. I'm married, Roy. Got hitched when I was sixteen. I'm staying here. But the folks want to take you and the others to California."

"Why should I go?" said Roy sharply, wiping a tomato on his tee shirt. "I already got a home with the Sheltons."

"Don't you want to be with your brothers and your sister Joy again?" asked Pansy. She pushed a strand of damp hair back from her round face. "C'mon, Roy. Go with us. We're just going somewhere now to talk, work things out. Please come."

Roy bit into the tomato. It was sour, too firm. He spit it out. A sudden blast of the horn sounded from the pickup.

"Dad's waiting," said Pansy. She waved toward the truck and shouted, "Just a minute!"

"It's no good," said Roy shortly. "I don't want to be with *her*." Pansy looked puzzled. "Her? You mean Mom?"

"Yeah. I don't want to be in the same room with her."

Pansy gazed anxiously from Roy to the truck. "Listen, Roy," she said finally, clasping his arm. "If you go back with the folks I'll work it out so you won't have to see Mom. I'll have the kids warn you when she's coming. I'll figure something. Give it a chance."

Roy pitched the tomato to the ground and plodded sullenly toward the truck. "A chance," he muttered. "That's all."

That day it was decided. The Comstocks would become a family again.

A month later, on July 3, 1953, Bertha Comstock, sixteen-year-old Joy, and the twins took a Greyhound bus from Salt

Lake City to Wilmington, California. By midmorning the scorching desert air blew through the open windows. Roy, thirsty and uncomfortable, sat with Ray on one side of the bus while Mom and Joy sat on the other. No contact with Mom—that was the way Roy wanted it.

They rode the bus late into the night and arrived in Wilmington in time for breakfast on July 4. Howard, who had returned the month before to rent a house for the family, welcomed them with bacon, eggs, and coffee. Bill and Richard, who had hitchhiked because there wasn't enough money for everyone to take the bus, had already arrived the night before.

At breakfast Howard said, "You know I got a job working the wheat fields near Torrance, operating a combine. Well, there's plenty of work for you guys, too. How about it?"

Bill said sure; Richard nodded. Roy and Ray exchanged uncertain glances. Howard helped himself to some more bacon. "You twins can ride the combine with me today if you want." He looked at Roy. "You ever been on a big piece of machinery like that?"

"No," said Roy. "You mean we can ride on it with you?"

"Sure. There's room. You'll like it."

After breakfast the twins climbed into the pickup and rode out to the field with their father. They spent the day on the combine, threshing wheat, feeling the power of the machine under them, the penetrating warmth of the California sun, and the dry rising whirlwinds of dirt and chaff tinting the air brown. As the day wore on, Roy's defensiveness dissipated. Maybe his dad wasn't so bad after all.

Every day that first week the boys ran the combine with their dad. Howard introduced his sons to everyone he knew, announcing with unmistakable pride, "These are my twins." It was a curious feeling for Roy, realizing he was this man's own flesh and blood.

On Saturday morning Howard said offhandedly, "You guys going out on the combine with me?"

Ray nodded, but Roy said, "No, I'm going to church."

Howard looked dumbfounded. "Church? On Saturday?"

Roy groped for words. "The Sheltons—they took us to church every Saturday. We never missed."

"Well, you're here now," said Howard. "So wouldn't you

rather be with Ray and me on the combine than go to church?"
"No, sir."
Howard was growing impatient. "So what church is it?"
"Seventh-Day Adventist."
Howard looked at Ray. "Is that where you go too?"
"No, I'm Mormon," said Ray. "I go to church on Sunday."
"And you'll be going every Sunday, I suppose?"
"Yes, sir, I sure will."
"So will I!" shouted Joy from the kitchen.
Howard threw up his hands in exasperation, then stalked out the door to his pickup.

Even Roy wasn't sure why he felt so strongly about going to church. It had something to do with the Sheltons, with his unwavering conviction that they were still his people, his real family. He had a feeling that no matter what happened, the Sheltons would always have his loyalty.

Aunt Verna had encouraged Roy to start a new life with his own family. "It's the right thing to do," she had said. Roy still wasn't convinced, but one thing he knew was that he didn't want to disappoint the Sheltons, even if it meant going to church every Saturday.

In the fall of 1953 Roy began eighth grade at Wilmington Junior High. Life settled into a predictable routine for the Comstocks. Although Roy tried to avoid his mother, it wasn't easy in a small house. When she asked him to do something, he obeyed, because the Sheltons had taught him to do as he was told. But he rarely spoke to her. In fact, he shared little of his life with either of his parents.

Both Roy and Ray resented their mother's unexpected overprotectiveness. She insisted on knowing where they were going, chided them for coming in late, and expected them to kiss her good night. Perhaps because she had so many years to make up for, she took her mothering role very seriously. Bill, Richard, and Joy were nearly old enough to be on their own, but she thought of the twins, only fourteen, as her "babies."

Roy felt that having survived ten years without a mother, he certainly didn't need one now. What right did she have to give orders and expect affection? Still Roy showed her a grudging surface respect and tried to keep his bitterness to himself.

There were other adjustments for Roy to make too, like

getting reacquainted with his brothers and sister. He had always been something of a loner, so he tended to hang back from the others, to go his own way. Even his closeness with his brother Ray became increasingly marred by the family's tendency to compare him unfavorably with his twin.

"Why can't you be more like Ray?" came the familiar refrain. Ray, with his quiet, agreeable temperament, was the good guy, never getting into trouble, always conscientious, considerate, and respectful. Roy, on the other hand, seemed to grate against people, ruffle feathers, create minor crises. It wasn't deliberate. He just stirred more commotion where he walked.

He sensed that he was still an outsider, and he knew it was probably his own fault. He wasn't making enough effort to adjust, to fit in. His bitterness toward his mother was putting a wedge between himself and the rest of the family. He saw it in their attitude, even in their teasing.

Sometimes Joy would say, "You know, Ray's my favorite brother." Then glancing at Roy she would add, "When Ray was born we *found* you."

Usually Richard would chime in with some cute remark, like, "Yeah, we scraped you up off the doorstep."

Roy laughed off the jokes, but he couldn't forget them. What was wrong with him that he couldn't measure up, couldn't please people? He himself wondered, *Why can't I be more like Ray?*

Roy's sense of alienation was temporarily forgotten as the holiday season approached. Christmas of 1953 proved to be the high point of the Comstocks' stay in Wilmington. Howard and his brood made frequent trips to Hemet where they picked mistletoe and hauled bushels of the festive greenery back in their pickup. Then they gathered, laughing and talking, and packaged the mistletoe in plastic bags to sell around the neighborhood, in shopping areas, at swap meets, and on street corners.

Roy enjoyed the laughter, the jokes, the excitement of Christmas, and the anticipation of earning some spending money. He didn't even mind Ray poking fun at him: "Did you hear what happened yesterday when we sold mistletoe door to door? This gorgeous lady invited Roy inside, then grabbed him and kissed him. Boy, *I'm* never that lucky!"

On Christmas day Roy and Ray sat outside in their tee shirts eating ice cream cones and marveling over the green grass and sunshine. They had to agree: Christmas was never like this before!

In January, 1954, the Comstock family moved to 11611-208th Street in Artesia, where the twins began attending Faye Ross School. Shortly after the move, Bill married Veronna, a girl he had met and dated in Wilmington. Howard Comstock started his own landscaping business and invited Pansy's husband, Everett Johnson, to help him. Pansy and Everett moved from Salt Lake City into a white stucco house down the street from the Comstocks.

Roy was dismayed to find that their house on 208th Street was just as cramped and cluttered as the house in Wilmington. It had a small living room and kitchen, two bedrooms (Howard and Bertha occupied one and Joy the other), and a porch at the back where Richard slept.

Roy and Ray occupied a room behind the garage, separate from the house. This arrangement made it easier for Roy to avoid his mother and to come and go as he pleased.

The furniture in the house was old: a maroon chair with rough, nubby fabric and torn armrests; a couch with lumps and loose springs; a maple table piled high with newspapers and magazines. In the kitchen was a linoleum-top table with red vinyl chairs. On the back porch sat a wringer washing machine. A network of clotheslines ran from the house to the edge of a large vegetable and flower garden that Howard carefully cultivated.

Roy shunned any idea of helping around the house. He never had liked housework, even at the Sheltons', so it was easy enough to fall into the habit of letting stuff pile up and leaving things where they dropped. It was a kind of rebellion, this deliberate carelessness. After all, if his mother didn't care how the place looked, if *nobody* cared, why should he?

But it wasn't just his mother's lax housekeeping that bothered Roy; it was his parents' standard of living—their small crackerbox house compared with the Sheltons' roomy, immaculate home. His tastes were still the Sheltons' tastes. How was he to go about reconciling his upper-middle-class conditioning with this low-income environment?

One way he tried to rise above his surroundings was by practicing the good grooming habits Aunt Verna had taught him—hair combed, clothes pressed, shoes polished. When his jeans were washed, he always got out the ironing board and pressed them. Never mind that his brothers scoffed and called him stupid.

Usually Roy saw his family only at mealtimes. When he came in for dinner there was always a large pot on the stove with stew, chicken, or a roast. Mom had a habit of throwing everything into one pot—meat, potatoes, vegetables, leftovers. The menu varied, but everything tasted the same. Roy heard that his mother had worked for a while in a diner and as a cook on a ranch. Her cooking tasted like camp food all right. But she made the best bread Roy ever ate.

Once in a while the family ate a meal together, but more often they ate on the run, each helping himself from the pot on the stove. When Howard's landscaping business kept him working overtime, he would come in late, sit down, have a cup of coffee, and gulp some bread and leftovers.

Whenever Roy walked in on his father eating alone, silent over his coffee, or when he saw Bill or Richard standing over the stove eating a bowl of stew, he flinched inside. He couldn't help remembering dinnertime at the Sheltons'—gleaming silverware, a balanced meal laid out on a white tablecloth, pleasant conversation and laughter, a feeling of oneness. It hadn't meant that much to Roy then, but *now*—

One fact was becoming evident to Roy. He had to find a way to fill his life, to take up his time so that he wouldn't have to hang around the house. He needed friends, a place to go, things to do—anything to keep him away from home.

CHAPTER NINE

One morning in late winter, 1954, Roy awoke, swung his legs over the side of the bed, and put his feet down in ice-cold water. He stared incredulously around the room. Water stood two feet deep.

"Ray, look!" he cried.

Ray peered down from his upper bunk. "Hey, everything's soaked!"

Sloshing through the water to get his clothes, Roy gasped, "I heard the rain beating on the roof last night, but I never figured it'd come inside."

"With all the water in here, I wonder how it looks in the house?"

They waded through knee-deep water to the house where they found the rooms flooded and the furniture water-soaked, ruined. Yet everyone else was still asleep. They slogged toward the bedrooms, shouting their grim news. "Mom! Dad! Joy! We're flooded!"

What Roy would remember most about the Artesia flood was not the damage it caused but the fun he and Ray had. They spent the day and most of the night helping the National Guard with rescue operations. While the Guard may have been oblivious of their heroic efforts, Roy and Ray, charged with energy and excitement, floated through the streets of Artesia in a borrowed rubber raft, helping stranded people out of their homes. It was a nice feeling—being brave, helping people, saving the community from the flood—even if some of Roy's heroism was only in his own imagination.

But the flood was only one moment of glory and adventure in an otherwise bleak existence. The way Roy saw it, life at home was still povertyville. He had to find a way of escape.

In the fall Roy began his freshman year at Artesia High, a brand-new school on the corner of Del Amo and Norwalk. But Roy had entered more than a new school; he had stepped unknowingly into a whole new world, a society on the verge of adulthood. He was surrounded by students preoccupied with dating, cars, sports, and grades. Here were attractive coeds in bouffant skirts and sweaters with angora collars or neck scarves—girls wearing pop beads and tangerine lipstick, gossiping about the sock hop or the latest Tony Martin disc. And guys wearing peg-leg pants and leather jackets, carefully combing their flattops or drakes, swapping information about their 1948 Chevy or custom 1951 Ford.

It occurred to Roy that perhaps here was his escape. He could become one of *them*, one of the crowd. He would belong. But it was easier said than done. Roy at fifteen was still a boy—slim, almost too thin, with shoulders that tended to droop. His angular face was accented by warmly vulnerable, wide-set eyes and a tentative smile.

Old feelings of inferiority constantly resurfaced, causing him to mumble in speech class, to walk with his head down, and to avoid unnecessary association with his classmates. He wondered how he could possibly measure up to the other students on campus. After all, he was just a Comstock.

One day after school Roy and an acquaintance—a thin, dark-haired boy with a permanent scowl—hitchhiked up Pioneer Boulevard to the Lookout Drive-in Restaurant in Norwalk. They ordered Cokes, then sat at an outside table.

"My brother always comes here," the youth told Roy.

"Yeah? How come?"

"He belongs to the Sinners Car Club. They meet here. Ain't you ever heard of the Sinners?"

"No," said Roy. He followed his friend's gaze over to several cars where a group of older boys stood talking. They wore jeans and leather jackets, the back of each boasting the word "Sinner" over an ominous skull and crossbones dripping blood. "I don't think I ever saw those guys at school," Roy remarked.

" 'Course not," snapped the boy. "They're at least nineteen or twenty. They quit school. They say school's just for kids."

Roy sipped his Coke. "So what do they do?"

"They rumble with the Roadrunners, their rival gang. They stomp 'em good. The Sinners are real tough dudes."

One of the gang members spotted the boys and ambled over. "Hey, little kid, what are you doin' hangin' around here?" he drawled. "Why don't you go home?"

The boy hunched his shoulders and snarled, "I don't have to. My brother's over there."

"So who's your friend?" said the older youth, nodding toward Roy. He lit a cigarette and placed it between his lips. "You got a mind to join the Sinners, huh, kid?"

Roy shook his head uncertainly. "No, uh, I don't know—"

"Maybe you wanta meet the rest of the guys first, huh?" He chuckled and winked at a fellow in a grimy tee shirt with rolled sleeves who had joined them. "What say we take these cats up to the clubhouse and show 'em around?"

The youth, a tall, thin blond with a red goatee and a network of tattoos on his arms, nodded approvingly. "Sure, man. We can always use another Sinner or two."

The first youth pushed his cigarette over to one side of his mouth and said, "I'm Mick and this here is Eddie. He's Tony's right-hand man. Ain't you his right-hand man, huh, Eddie?"

"Who's Tony?" asked Roy.

Eddie laughed menacingly. "Who's Tony? He don't know who Tony is! He just better come upstairs with us, huh, Mick?"

Reluctantly Roy followed the boys upstairs to a room over the Lookout Drive-in, a place little more than a storage room with boxes and crates. A dozen guys sat around, leather-jacketed replicas of Mick and Eddie. Most were drinking beer, smoking, or making small talk. Others kept time to the rhythm and blues music piped over the drive-in's loudspeaker.

"You like that Harlem beat?" Eddie asked Roy.

"It's OK." The closeness of the smoke-filled room, a sense of excitement mingled with fear, and the cacophony of sounds assaulted Roy's senses; he felt momentarily dizzy. He gazed around in wonderment until his eyes settled on a huge broad-shouldered man who had just come in the door. Immediately the room grew quiet.

"That's Tony," hissed Mick.

Tony was like no one Roy had ever seen before—a gruff giant with a pot belly and monstrous arms. His face was round and clean-shaven, with a deep scar over one eye, and his long straight black hair was tied back in a ponytail with a piece of rope. When he spoke, his voice was low, gravelly. "Eddie," he growled, pointing toward a case of beer in the corner.

Eddie sprang into action and handed Tony a beer. Tony tipped up the bottle, guzzled, then wiped his mouth in a quick, brusque motion. "You cats set for a rumble at the traffic circle tonight?" he said.

"Yeah, I got my chains," responded one ducktailed youth.

"I got my knife," said someone else.

"We'll tear them Roadrunners apart!" shouted another.

Mick nudged Roy. "How about it, kid? You wanta go with us tonight on the big fight?"

Roy stepped back unsteadily toward the door. "Oh, no, no thanks," he said quickly. "I—I gotta get home."

Roy was relieved to escape the cramped smoky room over the drive-in. He hadn't been too sure what the Sinners might do to him. They seemed afraid of nothing. How Roy wished he could be as brave and fearless as they. *Fat chance of that,* he thought dismally.

But something happened inside him that evening. He caught a vision he couldn't even put into words. He couldn't help feeling a grudging admiration for the Sinners. Strong and powerful, they could take care of themselves; yet they had treated him OK. On his way home he repeated his buddy's words: "They're real tough dudes!"

CHAPTER TEN

From time to time throughout Roy's freshman year he encountered various members of the Sinners Car Club—at the Lookout Drive-in, in a movie, on the street. The curious thing was that they remembered him and were always friendly. "Hey, kid, let me get you a Coke," one would say. Or, "You're cool, kid. Why don'tcha come with us?"

The Sinners were the only ones who seemed to be reaching out to Roy. There was no one at home or in school, not even Ray, with whom he felt comfortable or could build a relationship. And he had long since stopped attending church.

But during this year one person did enter Roy's life to exert a powerful influence. One day as Roy shuffled along the campus with his head down, William Atkins, dean of boys, approached and said, "What are you looking for, young man?"

Roy looked up, puzzled. "I'm not looking for anything."

"Then why are you staring at the ground?"

Roy grinned sheepishly. "I guess I always walk like that."

Mr. Atkins, a large, pleasant, full-faced man, returned the smile. "No student here at Artesia has to mope around like that. Remember, you're somebody. You can be anything you want to be. Keep that in mind and you'll do OK."

Roy's first meeting with Mr. Atkins was far from his last. Whenever he got into trouble for fighting or for throwing spitballs in class, he would be sent to the dean's office. There he would sit across from Mr. Atkins and stare sullenly at his shoes.

It amazed Roy that Mr. Atkins was invariably optimistic. "You know, Roy," he would begin, tapping his pencil lightly on the desk. "You don't have to get into trouble. I've watched you and you're not that kind of person. You can be a leader if you want to be. You've got the ability. Why don't you get involved in student body activities? Or try out for sports?"

Mr. Atkins' words began to work on Roy. Was it possible that he really could accomplish something? Could he show his family that he was as good as Ray?

Taking Mr. Atkins' advice, during his sophomore year Roy joined the Cavaliers and Frontiersmen—two school service organizations which planned dances, assemblies, intra-mural sports activities, and the football queen contest. And now Roy, having filled out and matured, also played right guard in varsity football and was a member of the Pioneer Varsity track team.

But Mr. Atkins' influence on Roy didn't stop there. Whenever the two met he encouraged Roy with, "You're doing fine. Keep up the good work." Then one day as Roy sat in his office, Mr. Atkins said, "How about going with me to the Kiwanis Club sometime? Learn something about community affairs. Maybe you'll pick up some ideas we could use here at school."

Although Roy couldn't imagine why Mr. Atkins wanted him, he agreed to go. He admired this man too much to risk disappointing him.

During the school year Roy's family moved into a tiny house in Hawaiian Gardens, an area he mockingly referred to as "Cesspool Acres." Seine Street was a dirt road deeply rutted with chuckholes. When the weather was dry, dust would blow into the house and settle on everything. During rainy seasons the road became a river of mud.

Even though Roy's brother Richard had married and moved out, the new house was intolerably crowded. Because Roy no longer had the privacy of a room separate from the rest of the family, he spent more and more time at the Lookout Drive-in, swapping stories with the guys and listening to the rock-and-roll music that was quickly replacing rhythm and blues in popularity. The Sinners, by accepting him as he was, bolstered Roy's precarious self-image. They listened to what he had to say, let him drink a little beer, and promised him he could join their car club when he got his own set of wheels.

Shortly after the move to Seine Street, Roy began working after school as a shelf boy at Parker's Hardware. Often after work he would hitchhike up to the Lookout to spend a couple of hours with the Sinners, then catch a ride home. When his mother asked where he had been, his stock reply was, "I had to work late at Parker's."

One afternoon during the second semester of Roy's sophomore year, Mr. Atkins stopped him in the hall and said, "I have something I'd like to talk to you about. Stop by my office after school."

Later, when they sat down together, Mr. Atkins sat back in his chair and gazed thoughtfully at Roy. "You're aware, aren't you, that Artesia is governed by the Community Coordinating Council?"

"Yes, sir, I guess so," said Roy.

"Well, how would you like to attend some of their meetings with me?"

Roy shrugged. "I don't know what I could—"

Mr. Atkins interrupted. "I'd like to start a youth coordinating council here at Artesia High. We need one, but I don't have anybody to head it. We need someone with real leadership ability."

"I see," Roy murmured. He didn't see at all.

"I think you could do it," said Mr. Atkins.

"Do it?" repeated Roy dumbly.

"Sure. Take charge. Help us set up a council here patterned after the community council. What do you say?"

Roy nodded reflexively. He had no idea what was involved in forming a council, but if Mr. Atkins wanted him for the job, he would get it done somehow.

In the days that followed, Roy worked with the Artesia Community Coordinating Council, a Kiwanis representative, and local youth clubs, to set up the proposed council. In May, 1956, the Youth Coordinating Council held its first meeting at Artesia High with the primary aim of promoting the ideas of youth in the community.

In June Roy, along with the secretary of the chamber of commerce and Artesia principal Richardson Hastings, met in conference with the county supervisor in Los Angeles. After the meeting Roy suggested they call on the Governor to thank him

for his support of the youth councils. Because of pressing obligations, California Governor Goodwin J. Knight was unable to
meet with the group, but he sent Roy a personal letter of regret.
Headlines in *The Californian,* the Artesia High newspaper, pro-
claimed: *STATE GOVERNOR WRITES LETTER TO YOUTH
HEAD.*

Reading the article, Roy was struck by how far he had come
in two years. To all appearances, he was no longer the meek,
mumbling, backward boy who first entered Artesia High. He had
become involved in school government, social and sports events,
and community affairs. Now both school and city officials
welcomed his opinions and considered him a valuable participant
in their projects. The Governor himself had taken time to write
Roy a letter.

But Roy felt little satisfaction inside. It was a sham, all of it. He
wasn't really a leader; he wasn't even a good citizen. It was a
game, carefully contrived and cleverly executed. He was acting
out a role—Mr. Nice Guy—to win peer and faculty approval. Inside he was the same scared, insecure guy he had always
been—the starry-eyed kid scaling a mountain to become Superman.

The only people Roy felt genuinely at ease with were members
of the Sinners Car Club. Here was his real world; this was where
he belonged. He met regularly now with the guys above the
Lookout Drive-in. Then in May, when his father gave him a 1946
Studebaker Champion for his seventeenth birthday, Roy became
an official member of the Sinners. But since his dilapidated
Champion wasn't considered a proper vehicle for a car club, he
usually drove another member's automobile—an Oldsmobile so
low to the ground that roller skates had been welded to the
frame to keep it from scraping the pavement.

Roy's unreserved commitment to the Sinners marked the
beginning of a radically different life-style. Now he was expected
to join in gang fights, to steal cars for the local fence, and to
break into the shops of the very merchants with whom he
worked in community projects. The gang's demands added a
sober new dimension to Roy's life, one he embraced as the necessary price of their acceptance and approval.

What Roy found both frightening and marvelous was that he
was able to maintain his incredibly divergent pursuits with few

qualms and only a minimum of inconvenience. The Sinners were mildly amused by Roy's "good guy" reputation while his school associates were aware only that the Sinners was a local car club. When Principal Hastings learned that Roy belonged to the Sinners, he remarked innocently, "It must be a good club if you're a member." And at a local conference the mayor of Lynwood put a comradely arm around Roy's shoulder and said fervently, "You know, we need more young people like you!"

Roy chuckled inside at the compliment and thought, *Boy, if he only knew the truth!* But the fact was, Roy was walking a perilous tightrope. He wondered how long it would be before his fragile illusion of accomplishment burst, before he lost his balance and took a fatal plunge.

CHAPTER ELEVEN

In the summer of 1956, between Roy's sophomore year and his junior year, an extraordinary happening touched the lives of the entire Comstock family. The drama began routinely enough on Thursday, August 2, while Roy's sister Joy Bell was staying with her mother-in-law Hazel Krebaum. The two women spent the afternoon chatting and watching television. The "Queen for a Day" show was on, and Jack Baily was introducing the next contestant when Joy went outside to hang out some clothes. She hurried back into the house when she heard Hazel calling her name. She found her mother-in-law sitting forward in her chair, watching the screen intently.

"Look at this," Hazel told Joy. "Doesn't that girl look like your sister Pansy?"

Joy gazed at the young woman. Indeed, she did look amazingly like Pansy—a well-rounded, full-faced girl with striking dark hair, the same distinctive chin, and a generous smile. "Who is she?" asked Joy.

"Her name's Eulah Marie," replied Hazel. "Isn't that the name of your half-sister who was kidnapped?"

"That was nearly thirty years ago," said Joy. "How could—?"

Hazel raised her hand. "Listen. She's telling her story."

The television camera moved in for a closeup on the contestant. "Until I was eighteen I thought my parents were

John and Lola Jones," said the girl. "Then I found out I wasn't a
Jones at all. My natural parents gave me up when I was two.
Their name was Jewett. For over twelve years now I've tried to
locate them, to find out who they are . . . and who I am." Her
soft voice quavered momentarily. "I have a special reason for
wanting to find them now. I recently became a Mormon and I
need my birth certificate so I can fill out my church membership
records correctly."

Joy reached for her mother-in-law's arm. "She said *Jewett.*
That's the name of mother's first husband!"

"She must be your sister," murmured Hazel in astonishment.

"What should I do?" asked Joy.

Hazel stood up. "Call the TV station. Maybe they'll let us talk
to her."

Joy reached for the phone. Her hand was trembling. "It's the
NBC studios in Hollywood. But I'm too nervous to call."

Hazel took the phone from her. "I'll make the call."

Moments later, Hazel Krebaum was speaking with Dick
Robbins, writer for the "Queen for a Day" show. When he
learned the reason for her call, he brought Eulah Marie to the
phone. Hazel heard a gentle, tentative voice say, "Hello, this is
Eulah Marie Hoppock."

Hazel was breathless, her voice breaking with excitement.
"Hello. I—I'm calling because I think my daughter-in-law is your
sister . . . and I know where your mother is."

There was a pause, then the girl spoke, her voice swelling with
emotion. "Please tell me, how—how can I reach you?"

"I'm Hazel Krebaum from Paramount, California. But, here, let
me put my daughter-in-law on."

Joy took the phone. She felt as if she were walking and talking
in a dream. "Hello, Eulah Marie? My mother—she had a little girl
named Eulah Marie. She was born August 1, 1925."

The young woman responded eagerly, "*My* name is Eulah
Marie and *I* was born August 1, 1925."

"My mother's little girl was kidnapped when she was almost
two," Joy continued.

There was a slight gasp. "Kidnapped? No, it couldn't be! My
parents gave me away—"

"My mother never gave her daughter away," replied Joy. "Her
child was taken by a couple who were caring for her."

The girl's voice wavered. "Please, when can I see you?"

"Today?" suggested Joy. "If you can pick me up here in Paramount, I'll take you to our mother."

"Our mother," the girl breathed solemnly, almost a prayer. Joy could scarcely hear her.

Late that afternoon Eulah Marie and her two children, six-year-old Brenda Susan and four-year-old Delman Wayne, arrived at the Krebaum home. After nervous, happy introductions had been made, Joy told Eulah that "Queen for a Day" wanted her to call them right away. Eulah telephoned and learned that several calls had come in for her from Salt Lake City. "Those calls are from my relatives," Joy told her excitedly. "Our relatives."

Shortly the three women drove through Artesia toward Hawaiian Gardens, on their way to the little house on Seine Street where Bertha Comstock lived.

"Does she know I'm coming?" Eulah asked.

"No," said Joy. "I thought we should tell her in person. She has a bad heart."

"I'm sorry," said Eulah, then added, "There's so much I want to know about all of you."

"We want to know about you too," said Joy.

Eulah smiled. "I'll try to fill you in before we reach the house. When I was eighteen I was with some friends in a cafe and we were all talking about who we looked like. This old family friend spoke up and told me, 'You don't look like a Jones because you aren't a Jones.' I was speechless. I went to my grandmother who had raised me since my folks' divorce. She told me it was true. Her son John and his wife Lola had gotten me in Salt Lake City. Later, when I saw my father, he told me my natural parents had given me to him when they were divorced. I wasn't even three when John and Lola were also divorced, so I never knew my foster mother. I spent several years trying to find Lola. When I finally contacted her, she wrote and told me my real name was Jewett."

"It really sounds complicated," said Joy. "How did you get the idea of going on 'Queen for a Day'?"

Eulah kept her eyes on the traffic as she answered. "An acquaintance suggested I go on the television program and present my problem. My husband was on a fishing trip, so the children and I drove from Bartlesville, Oklahoma, out here to California."

"What was it like getting on the show?" asked Joy.

Eulah laughed heartily. "For several days, maybe four, I had to stand in line trying to get a ticket. I kept going back. And I had to find a baby-sitter for the children. One day I was chosen for the show, but I still didn't get on the program. But today I made it!"

"You were runner-up to the queen, weren't you?" remarked Hazel.

Eulah nodded. "I didn't mind not winning. My husband is a builder and developer. I don't need the money or the prizes. I just wanted the chance to tell my story on national television. I prayed someone would see me and know who I was. God answered my prayer."

"It looks like he answered ours too," said Joy.

"Please, tell me more about the family," urged Eulah.

"Well, you have five brothers and two sisters," Joy told her.

Eulah shook her head in disbelief. "I thought I was an only child," she marveled, her voice tremulous. "I've always wanted brothers and sisters!"

When they pulled up in front of the little house on Seine Street, Joy said apologetically, "The house isn't much, but the folks plan to move into a nicer place any time now, if Dad's landscaping business does better."

Joy opened the car door and stepped out, then looked back at Eulah. "Will you wait a few minutes? We need to prepare Momma."

Eulah nodded. She had waited all her life. A few minutes more wouldn't matter.

Hazel and Joy soon reappeared. They escorted Eulah into the house and asked her to be seated. She glanced around self-consciously at several strangers, then sat on one end of the couch.

"Momma will be in shortly," said Joy.

Moments later someone touched Eulah on the shoulder. She turned to gaze into eyes very much like her own. Bertha Comstock, now a frail, white-haired woman in her early fifties, sat down on the arm of the couch. Eulah laid her head in Bertha's lap and wept.

A young woman who looked much like Eulah herself came over and put her arms around Bertha. "Now, Momma, don't get excited," she said soothingly. "It might not be Eulah Marie."

Eulah raised her head, her face wet with tears. "How many Eulah Maries are looking for their mothers?" she asked.

Bertha, her eyes glistening, gazed from her daughter Pansy back to Eulah. "She looks like my side of the family. She's an Armstrong," she said firmly, smiling. Handing Eulah a picture of a man and woman, she added, "This is for you. See, your name's right there. It's your Grandma and Grandpa Jewett. I saved it for you all these years."

Bertha also gave Eulah a special keepsake—a note she had written to her back in 1947. It read, "My dear daughter Eulah, dearest little girl. When you were little I had you close by. Someone wished to care for you. One evening I came to see you and you were so pretty, sweet, and clean. That was the last I saw you, for the people took you away without my knowing. How I missed you and yearned for you through the years, for now, my darling, you are twenty-two and I know not where you are. If I could just see you and know you are happy and just as sweet as ever, I'd be a very happy person. I'll keep this and someday you may come for me."

After a few minutes Joy introduced Eulah to Pansy and her

husband Everett, and to two of her brothers, Richard and Ray.
Later that evening she would meet Roy and her stepfather,
Howard Comstock.

Pansy smiled and said, "I had a doll named Eulah Marie.
Momma used to tell us stories about you, but we kids thought
they were fairy tales. We didn't know you were real."

"And I didn't know any of you even existed," replied Eulah.

The family spent the evening making telephone calls to
relatives near and distant, sharing the incredible news of the
reunion between Bertha and her long-lost daughter.

In confidence Bertha talked to Eulah about her two early
losses—her oldest daughter, her youngest son—and of the effect
on her life. "It was worse for me with you," she said soberly.
"With Johnnie it was final. But you—I never knew where you
were or how you were being treated."

For seventeen-year-old Roy it was not just the reunion that
mattered; for him it was a thrilling moment of encouragement to
realize that a member of his family had broken the pattern of
poverty and failure. If his half sister could do it, perhaps there
was a chance for Roy too.

The next day, reporters and photographers swarmed over the
Comstock home, asking questions and taking pictures. Local
newspapers carried the story. *The Desert News*, a Salt Lake
City paper, conducted an interview by phone. That afternoon
Eulah met her brother Bill and his family. Milt, in the Navy in
San Francisco, requested a five-day leave, and he and his family
arrived early the next morning. Eulah's husband cut his fishing
trip short and flew in from Oklahoma. That afternoon relatives
from the entire Los Angeles area converged on Seine Street,
making a total of fifty newfound relatives. Later, in Salt Lake
City, Eulah would encounter another twenty-two relatives on her
mother's side. Still later she would locate Frank Jewett, her
natural father, and discover several more brothers and a sister.

The following Monday, the entire Comstock clan appeared on
the "Queen for a Day" show. Ben Alexander, standing in for
Jack Baily, introduced mother and daughter to the TV audience.
It was a spectacular conclusion to a long and mysterious drama
that had begun twenty-nine years before with the abduction of a
two-year-old child. But for Bertha Comstock and Eulah Marie,
this day wasn't an ending. It was a miraculous new beginning.

CHAPTER TWELVE

As his junior year of high school began, Roy was too absorbed in his own endeavors to give much thought to his mother's reunion with her long-lost daughter Eulah. Roy entered unreservedly into school affairs as well as gang activities. School by day; the gang by night. Two distinct, opposing life-styles.

As student body director of activities at Artesia High, Roy was in charge of organizing special dances, pep rallies, and school assemblies. Maintaining his friendship with Dean of Boys William Atkins, Roy delved further into student government and eventually became president of the Youth Coordinating Council for the state of California. He was also appointed to serve on Governor Knight's youth advisory commission on the prevention of juvenile delinquency.

This was a subject on which Roy was able to speak with impressive authority. And why not? He was on the verge of assuming leadership of the Sinners Car Club. When it came to assessing the problems of juvenile delinquents, Roy had firsthand knowledge. He knew how guys like Mick and Eddie thought, what made them tick. Maybe that explained the gradual shifting of the Sinners' loyalty from Tony to himself.

The way Roy had it figured, gang leadership should be a matter of brains, not brawn. Tony was a big, tough guy, but he didn't think clearly; he was slow and sometimes incoherent. Gradually Roy started planning more and more of the gang's activities—a poker run, a fight at the traffic circle, a rollicking party with the Saints, their sister club.

The guys unthinkingly accepted Roy's leadership. Roy never directly challenged Tony; the two never fought. They didn't have to. Tony, who evidently still considered Roy a harmless kid, was oblivious of Roy's growing popularity with the guys. Before Tony knew it, Roy had passed him. Without striking a blow, Roy had won the gang's allegiance. Only Eddie remained blindly faithful to the former leader. If Tony said, "Go fight that guy over there," Eddie would fight for all he was worth. Even if he got his teeth knocked in, Eddie would stumble back, blabbering, "Hey, Tony, I really got him, huh, Tony, huh?"

Roy had little patience with such mindless violence. Fighting didn't appeal to him; he considered it a necessary evil for defending the club and maintaining the Sinners' status among rival gangs. He much preferred using his cunning.

But when Roy faced a contest with another gang leader, he couldn't avoid fighting. When he fought, he fought dirty because he didn't know how to fight clean. A part of him was afraid to fight. He had no confidence in his arms. But he could use his feet. He could kick the life out of a guy if he had to. One evening he almost did.

After finishing early at Parker's Hardware, Roy had driven over to the Lookout Drive-in. There in the twilight, pinstriped cars flanked the building like metal appendages, and pretty carhops in breezy skirts delivered trays of hamburgers and shakes. The loudspeaker was on full blast. The radio deejay's sleek, slippery voice crooned, "This is station K-DAY bringing all you boppers your favorite new hillbilly rock-and-roll artist Elvis the Pelvis, singing 'Don't Be Cruel.' If you cats can't bop to this, you're a square from nowhere!"

Roy's buddy Mick appeared out of the shadows and handed him a beer. "Let's cut outta here, man, and go find us some Saints. I got the car loaded with beer, slow gin, and 7-up."

Roy waved off the beer. "Where are the guys?"

Mick shrugged. "Upstairs, I guess. Why?"

"We got trouble. Eddie and some of the boys set fire to the Roadrunners' clubhouse."

Mick swallowed his surprise. "You mean that old warehouse next to the funeral home?"

Roy nodded. "Now they wanta rumble. We've got twenty minutes to meet them at the circle."

Mick followed Roy upstairs. "They deserved the fire, Roy, the way they beat the stuffin' outta Buckeye last week."

Roy opened the hangout door and gazed around the room. "Come on, guys, let's make dust. It's a showdown with the Roadrunners."

A half hour later a dozen cars were parked on the side streets around the Long Beach traffic circle. Roy stood facing the rival leader—a tall, broad-shouldered bruiser brandishing a tire iron. The respective gangs formed tense, uneasy arcs behind the two opponents. It was customary for only the leaders to fight at first. Once a leader was down, the rest of the gang could strike.

But this was Roy's fight. He couldn't escape it. Fear left a sour taste in his mouth as he and his rival cautiously paced each other, their eyes riveted in chilling scrutiny. Roy had his first clue he could beat the guy when he spied fear in his eyes. Why, this poor sap was as terrified as Roy himself!

Momentarily Roy recalled the advice his brother Milt had given him years before: *If you're going to fight, get in the first blow.*

Without warning, Roy kicked his foe where it hurt. As the youth crumpled and fell, the Sinners cheered. "Stomp it out of him!" someone shouted. "Finish the job! Give it to him!"

Impulsively Roy stooped down and shoved the youth's open mouth against the curb. His foot came down hard on the back of the fellow's head.

A gasp rose from the Roadrunners. In an instant pandemonium broke out. Sinners and Roadrunners mixed in a bloody free-for-all amid heated shouts and curses. Over the chaos erupted the sudden scream of a siren. The rampaging youths halted in midair. Someone hissed, "Cool it! The cops! Let's lay rubber!"

They scattered in every direction—battered, leather-jacketed ruffians crowding into their autos and peeling off down residential side streets away from the threatening sirens.

Only when they had returned to the dim privacy of their Lookout hideaway did the troop breathe easily again. They sat around, smoked, had some beers, laughed, and joked. Roy drank eagerly, relieved that the tension in his muscles was finally dissipating.

"You were a real cool head," Mick told him approvingly. "You fixed that creep good."

"Yeah, sure," said Roy. "Check tomorrow and see how he's doing, OK?" He tipped up his bottle for another swallow. The liquid going down was cold and pleasantly biting. He felt good, elated, tough. Surely tonight he had proved he was someone to be reckoned with.

Later, driving home alone, Roy's spirits plunged. He felt depressed, empty, anxious. Guilt pressed in on him. He couldn't forget that kid's head on the curb . . . his own foot coming down.

"Oh, God, I could have killed him!" he acknowledged in disbelief. He felt a sudden revulsion in the pit of his stomach, a raw nausea that rocketed to his throat. He thought he might vomit. Defensively he turned up the radio, submerging himself in a pulsating sea of sound.

In bed that night Roy stared for long hours into the darkness, still stunned by his earlier rash assault. Silent accusations taunted him: *It was wrong . . . stupid . . . brutal, stepping on that poor oaf. Maybe you killed him. Imagine, Roy Comstock, a murderer! What would the Sheltons say if they could see you now?*

But by morning the guilt had faded. Roy rose early and left for school, his mind absorbed with ideas for a report he had to prepare for the Governor's commission on the prevention of juvenile delinquency. He wondered what he should title it. With a wry chuckle he decided on "Proposed Methods for Keeping Delinquents off the Streets."

Roy had other obligations today too. He had to plan the agenda for the Youth Coordinating Council meeting this afternoon. The group intended to submit certain propositions to the community council—the need for a traffic light at a busy intersection near the school, a request for more money for park equipment, and a proposal for involving students in the support of a local bond issue. Roy recalled, too, that he had to work on his campaign for second semester student body president. It was an office he wanted to win.

By the time Roy arrived at school, the transition was complete; he had shifted gears mentally from scrapping, boozing hellion to diligent student and assertive community leader. His "good boy" facade was in place; he was ready to tackle the day.

In leadership class that morning Roy stood up and presented his ideas for the annual Artesia fair and parade. "It's not till the end of May," he said, looking around the room from face to face. The boys sat there in their Ivy League shirts, denim slacks, and suede shoes. The girls smiled confidently in their sheath dresses or stylish sweaters and tweed skirts.

Roy glanced down at his own patched jeans and worn shoes and wondered momentarily why he was standing here playing the big shot. And why were his classmates listening attentively, ready to take his suggestions? "We're putting on a talent show this year," he continued, collecting his thoughts. "I figure we should charge admission and get kids from the different school clubs to perform."

A pretty blonde raised her hand. "You mean like 'Ted Mack's Original Amateur Hour'?"

"Yeah, that's it," said Roy.

"But where can we hold it so people will come and see us?"

"I thought we could pitch a big tent at the fair, right where people pass by. We could build a stage and set up folding chairs."

"Crazy, man," whistled an auburn-haired boy with a crew cut.

Roy grinned. "You like that idea, Jim? Then how about you taking charge? Round up some of the guys and see what you can work out—permits, supplies, whatever we need for the tent. Then check back with me next week, OK?"

"But where are we going to find good talent?" quizzed a hefty brunette girl.

Roy thought a minute. "Evelyn, you could set up auditions among the various clubs. Appoint someone from each club to help you."

"Oh, wow, what a job!" she responded. "But I'll do my best."

Roy added, "We've got to think about the parade too. I believe we can make this the best one Artesia's ever had."

"I don't know, Roy," said Jim doubtfully. "The parade may be skimpy. Not all the participants have cars to drive."

"And some of our crates look pretty raunchy," added another boy. "It's too bad we don't all have shiny, brand-new wheels."

"Maybe we can," said Roy, an idea brewing. "I think I'll go visit some of the local dealerships."

"You think they'll hand over their cars just like that?"

"Maybe not," Roy admitted. "But for a little free advertising they might lend us their demos."

"Hey, man, that's the most!" chorused several students. "Just leave it to Comstock," said someone else. "He'll make things happen!"

Roy flashed a self-assured grin, but inside he felt uneasy. When would his classmates wake up and realize he wasn't half the leader he pretended to be? *A real leader wouldn't pawn off all the work on others,* he told himself. He was always setting things in motion but never finishing anything himself. Sure, things usually worked out all right, but maybe it was just luck. Even when his projects were successful, he felt like a failure and a fraud. It would be several years before he would grasp the concept that a good leader always delegates responsibilities.

That evening Roy joined his comrades as usual in the room above the Lookout Drive-in. Mick was standing before a cloudy mirror, combing his ducktail. He kept combing, addressing Roy's reflection. "The guys wanta know when we're gonna pick up some parts for our cars. You know," he smirked, "at good ol' 'Midnight Auto Supply.'"

Roy unzipped his leather jacket. "Friday night," he answered. "Have Buckeye and Red make a list of what we need, then case the store during the day to see where the stuff is located."

"Cool," said Mick. He wiped his comb on his tee shirt and stuck it in his back pocket. "Sometimes I think that boss-guy moves stuff around in his store just to confuse us." He lit two cigarettes and handed one to Roy.

Roy took it, drew in, and exhaled slowly. "Remind Red we take only what we can carry to the end of the alley. Last time he took enough stuff to build himself a bus."

Mick nodded. "I'll tell him to limit it to mufflers, ornaments, hubcaps, stuff like that."

"Maybe a tire or two if he's good," said Roy. They both laughed.

Roy glanced over at several guys playing poker. "Where's Tony?"

"He and Eddie are delivering a car to Buzz—the '55 Chevy Coupe we picked up last week."

"OK," said Roy. "The heat should be off by now. Buzz better cough up a few hundred for that baby."

Roy took another drag on his cigarette. He didn't like Buzz, the skinny, bald, buzzard-beaked man who fenced the cars the Sinners stole. Old Buzz, with the beady rat-eyes and a thick smelly cigar planted between his lips, never let them forget that if he ever got nabbed, so would they. Even as he doled out cash for their latest trophy, he would cackle, "Remember, I got the goods on you, plenty!"

Roy wasn't especially fond of stealing cars or breaking into stores, but most of the Sinners—school dropouts without work—had no other livelihood. They had a painstaking routine for heisting autos. No stealing off parking lots; only residential cars. And they knew the market, knew what was in demand. Convertibles were popular—and easy to enter. Five, ten seconds it took. When a Sinner spotted what he wanted, he trailed the driver for days, got his address, observed his routine, watched his home. He would strike only when the moment was right, when he was sure of success.

Stolen cars were stored in a local garage for a few days until the heat was off; then they were delivered to Buzz, who always paid cash—anywhere from a hundred to a grand (though rarely that much). Buzz had his own outfit. His men would repaint the cars, file off the engine numbers and put on new license plates, then sell the vehicles to unsuspecting dupes.

Roy was putting out his cigarette when Tony and Eddie burst in, their faces flushed with excitement. "Buzz says he'll give us a grand if we find him an Imperial Convertible—one o' them push button beauties," Tony announced.

The poker game ended abruptly. "What are we waitin' for?" clucked one round, brawny-armed fellow. "Let's cruise."

Two hours later the Sinners swarmed back to their clubhouse to compare notes. Had anyone spotted an Imperial Convertible?

"There ain't no such car in all Artesia," grumped Eddie.

Buckeye broke in with, "I spied a real cool buggy—a custom Ford with a nosed and decked body and dual exhausts. Man, it sounded mellow!"

Mick took off his jacket, tossed it aside, and rolled his shirt sleeves while he talked. "I didn't spot our dreamboat either, but I found us a powder-blue rod channeled almost on the ground. The hood's shaved clean and it has two-foot headers and Buick flipper hubcaps."

"Forget it," said Tony. "Them custom jobs're too easy to trace."

"So what? I dig it. It's low and smooth, and decked out with silver tuck and roll seats. I just might pick it up for myself."

"Can it, will you!" exploded Tony. He shoved Mick backward and the two scuffled briefly until Red slammed open the door and exclaimed, "Hey, I spotted it—our silver slipper—over in Belmont Heights!"

Roy stepped forward and looked knowingly at his eager, skittish companions. "OK, fellas, sit back and relax. *This* baby's *mine!*"

The following Friday evening, Roy, a grand richer and still tasting sweet victory over his latest coup (snagging a perfect Imperial Convertible), met four of his cronies in an alley off Pioneer Boulevard in Artesia. Most of the old downtown stores had back doors with glass windows, making them easy targets for break-ins.

"Mick's posted at one end of the alley and Tony at the other," Roy told Buckeye and Red. "If you hear their whistle, drop everything and scram." He handed Red the flashlight. "Here. You checked the layout this morning, so you lead us to the stuff. We gotta be in and out in five minutes."

"OK, that's cool," murmured Red, snuffing out a cigarette with his heel.

They crept stealthily through the shadows toward the auto supply store. At the back door Red focused the narrow beam of light while Roy took a glass cutter and deftly scarred the window. Then he tapped lightly on the pane and it fell in with a brief tinkling clatter. Roy reached in and opened the door. Slipping inside, they padded noiselessly over the tile floor, following Red's darting oval of light. "Mufflers right here," he whispered. Then, "Tires are two aisles over, by the wall."

Minutes later the three youths, their arms laden with supplies, sprinted down the alley to their waiting car. They scrambled inside and peeled triumphantly out of the alley, up Pioneer Boulevard, back to Norwalk. Mission accomplished without a hitch!

It wasn't until the early hours of the morning, as Roy tossed and turned in bed, that the taste of victory began to lose its savor. Roy chided himself; he should have felt good about this week. He'd turned over an Imperial Convertible to Buzz and he'd replenished the club's auto supplies. And things were going better than ever at school. Things were cool!—until moments like this when, alone in the darkness, he had to face himself and ask, *Who am I?*

He was hiding so much from so many people. He couldn't risk forming any close relationships lest his family or school friends find out about his night life. And if he shared too much of his school life with the gang, they would make fun of him. Obviously he wasn't building anything in either place. It seemed to Roy that everything he did was out there, on the surface; he couldn't bring things—or people—in close. Nothing went deep; nothing was real.

"It's all going to disappear anyway," he murmured into his pillow. "Why shouldn't I end up with zero in life—just like Dad?"

Ray, in the upper bunk, rolled over and drawled sleepily, "You say something?"

"No," Roy answered huskily. "Nothing at all."

CHAPTER THIRTEEN

Early in May, 1957, Roy's perilously balanced dual world collapsed around him. Events were already unfolding as Roy sat in Mr. Littleton's English class, his mind straying from participles and verbs. Lately he had been doing a lot of thinking about his life and was beginning to believe he could make something of himself after all. Exerting a real effort to go straight, he hadn't heisted a car in nearly two months, nor had he commandeered any more robberies. Already he felt better about himself. Now if only he could live up to Mr. Atkins' image of him.

Without warning, a man entered the classroom, interrupting Mr. Littleton's lecture, and asked for Roy Comstock. The thin, bespectacled teacher pointed Roy out, and Roy stood up. As he followed the stranger down the hall, it didn't occur to Roy that trouble lay ahead. Even as they entered the principal's office, Roy assumed the fellow was someone from the Kiwanis Club or a local civic group wanting him to speak and share what the youth council was doing. Only when Roy spotted another sober-faced stranger and gazed into the sad, concerned eyes of Mr. Atkins did he sense the grim reality. Then his heart started pounding hard as a single terrifying word burned in his mind. *Caught!*

"We have a warrant for your arrest," the man told Roy, perfunctorily flashing a badge. "You are charged with ten counts of auto theft."

"I think you're going to find out you have the wrong boy," Mr. Atkins interjected.

"No, sir," replied the officer. "Roy Comstock has been identified as the leader of a gang we've been after for some time now."

Shortly the two plainclothesmen drove Roy to the Norwalk Police Station. He sat in silence, staring glumly out the car window, a hundred thoughts surging through his mind: the hurt and disappointment in Mr. Atkins' face just now; memories of the Sheltons (would they find out about his arrest?); his school responsibilities (he was supposed to give a speech in assembly tomorrow); and what about his future? Would everyone at school find out he had been busted? Would he be locked away in some cell for the rest of his life?

At the station where Roy was booked, officers fingerprinted him, took mug shots, then led him to a small, cheerless room where he was interrogated. There Roy was confronted with the alarming news that an older gang member had been caught and, in exchange for a lighter sentence, had turned over enough evidence to break the Sinners Car Club wide open. Realizing there was no way out, Roy quietly admitted his own guilt.

After taking down his statement, an officer placed Roy in a cell.

There Roy sat, numb with shock. Convinced he was in the throes of a nightmare, he wondered if he would ever wake up. He had to! He stared around at the confining walls and thought in desperation, *How can I get out of here? How can I escape?* There was a small barred window at the back of his cell. Ominous-looking bars stretched across the front. He was trapped—and very much alone.

By early evening Howard Comstock arrived, identified Roy, and filled out several official forms. Roy cringed inside, remembering how proud his father had been lately of his accomplishments at school. Now Howard approached Roy's cell, his expression grave. He stared in silent scrutiny for several moments, then said, "Did you really do what they say you did?"

Roy pulled his gaze away in shame. "Yeah."

Howard coughed harshly. "It's hard for me to believe you would do that."

There didn't seem to be much more to say. Roy and his dad never had talked much. It was as though they didn't even know each other; they just happened to be strangers in the same place at the same time. And how could Roy explain the irony that he had been caught too late, that he had just started getting his life together?

Before his father left, Roy said, "Dad, don't tell people where I'm at."

Howard's expression shifted slightly.

"Look, Dad," Roy pressed on urgently, "I don't want the family to know. Tell them I ran away. Tell them anything, but just don't tell them—about this!"

Howard turned away, his voice low, husky. "All right, Roy, if that's how you want it."

The big weather-beaten man shambled out. Roy watched him leave, and an ache formed in his throat. He yearned for the comfort that was never offered. His father had come and gone and it made no difference at all.

The next day Roy was transferred to Juvenile Hall in Los Angeles—a cold, gray, sterile building with rows of barred windows. He shared a room with several other boys.

One youth—a fat, foul-mouthed kid who looked barely old enough to shave—asked in a drawling, twangy voice, "What'd you get busted for?"

"I ripped off a couple cars," replied Roy.

"Oh, good, man!" The boy snickered, then added with obvious pride, "I got busted for rape."

Roy walked away in disgust. If this creep was an example of what lay ahead, the days were going to be long indeed!

After several days in Juvenile Hall, Roy appeared in court for sentencing. The judge asked how he pleaded and he answered, "Guilty."

The judge's brows lowered menacingly. "Next week you'll be eighteen years old, am I right?"

"Yes, sir," said Roy.

"Do you realize how close you came to being sentenced as an adult?"

"Yes, sir," Roy said again.

"Are you also aware that the usual juvenile sentence for your crime is ten years?" the judge continued. "You didn't merely take a car, drive it around, and leave it somewhere. You stole cars and sold them; that's an adult crime."

Roy swallowed hard. "Yes, sir."

The judge held up a sheet of paper. "You see this? It's a letter from someone who thinks very well of you—William Atkins. He gives you a strong recommendation. I see, too, that this is your first offense." He paused reflectively, his brow furrowed. Then he said, "I'm going to try you for all ten counts of auto theft together. That gives you a one-year term . . . which I'm reducing to ninety days at Camp Five in San Dimas—with a two-year probation period."

Roy was profoundly relieved to receive a light sentence, but at the same time anxious over what to expect at San Dimas. Camp Five was a large official-looking complex in the mountains, where convicted juveniles learned the art of fighting forest fires. The boys lived in barracks, ate in a cafeteria, and had access to recreational facilities that included a basketball court and Ping-Pong and pool tables. They spent many of their waking hours on training maneuvers, chopping back tangled brush, planting trees, and learning how to block fires by digging trenches and filling them with water from the irrigation lines.

Roy became a squad leader and participated in fighting several fires during his stay at San Dimas. He didn't mind the work. And the camp was comfortable and the food good—three square meals a day. One thing that bothered Roy about the place was the lack of privacy and the bawdy atmosphere in the large barracks (twenty-five to thirty beds and an open latrine). There were frequent fights, a lot of dirty language, and crude jokes about women. Roy, who had an aversion to vulgarity, avoided the scuffles and tried his best to shut out the profanity and smut.

Roy's greatest concern was that someone he knew would show up at Camp Five, recognize him, and take back word that he was serving time. He anxiously studied every new face, but not once in three months' time did he encounter anyone he knew from the outside world.

While at Camp Five, Roy fell into the habit of attending chapel services each Sunday. The only other option was trekking off somewhere to plant trees. Church was easier. Groups from many local congregations came in and put on programs, and

Roy found that he enjoyed the music. The songs reminded him of the days when he'd attended church with the Sheltons. He especially recalled singing, "What a Friend We Have in Jesus." It was a nice song; he liked it.

Sometimes he thought about God and the fact that he had done many things God wouldn't approve of. But more often he thought about the Sheltons and hoped they would never find out how badly he had turned out. Thinking of Mrs. Shelton, Roy's face would burn with shame. He remembered the time she had believed him over her own son. Roy had gloated then, but now the incident plagued him. *I shouldn't have done it,* he chided himself over and over. *I shouldn't have lied!*

In August Roy was released from Camp Five. Howard Comstock came for Roy and drove him home in his pickup truck. Roy could only marvel that it was good to be going home, good to be free.

At home there was little fanfare over Roy's return. Everyone supposed he had been visiting relatives in Oregon. Roy suspected that his mother knew the truth, but she never mentioned it and neither did he.

Ray greeted Roy with, "Well, how was Oregon?"

"OK," Roy replied. "I didn't do much. Just spent a lot of time in the woods and mountains."

"Yeah? Doing what?"

"I worked with some guys putting out forest fires. We dug trenches and planted trees, stuff like that."

Ray grinned. "Sounds like fun."

"Sure," mumbled Roy. "It was OK."

The subject didn't come up again.

CHAPTER FOURTEEN

For a brief time during 1957, Howard Comstock's landscaping business flourished enough that he was able to move his family into a nice house in Lakewood. But when Howard overextended himself, the business collapsed. By the time Roy arrived home from Camp Five, his parents and Ray occupied a cramped dwelling behind the Hardy Morrison home on Verne Street in Hawaiian Gardens.

The structure, which Roy tagged "the back house," was originally a chicken coop built with scrap lumber. Now gophers persistently gnawed through the rotting floorboards which lay directly on the ground. It was a comedown, even for the Comstocks, but it was all they could afford for a while. Howard and Bertha were both in failing health. Howard, who coughed constantly and was often too weak to work, augmented his meager income with a disability check. Bertha, increasingly frail, shook with a palsy.

Their landlords, the Morrisons, often took in Roy and Ray and fed them along with their own children. When the twins appeared at her door, Mrs. Morrison would chuckle and declare in her deep, warm, gravelly voice, "Come on in, boys, and have some lunch. I just brought home six gallons of milk from the dairy, so there's plenty. Got soup and crackers too."

Occasionally Roy dated Mrs. Morrison's daughter Vera, but more often he joined Vera's brothers for an afternoon playing Monopoly and consuming bowls of soup or stew.

Bertha Comstock would lament, "I just can't feed them two boys. I just can't!" And Mrs. Morrison would laugh good-naturedly and reply, "They're growin' youngsters just like my kids. I never saw no one could drink more milk or eat more soup and crackers than the bunch of 'em. But I don't mind a bit. Your boys are welcome anytime!"

In September when Roy began his senior year at Artesia High, he was immensely relieved to discover that none of the students knew about his arrest or the time he had served. Incredibly, he was able to resume his life as if nothing had happened.

During his first week back in school, Roy was called into the office of William Atkins, now principal of Artesia High. Roy dreaded facing Mr. Atkins again, but the former dean of boys welcomed him with a ready smile. "I just want to clear the air between us," he told Roy.

Roy sat down uncomfortably. "Yes, sir."

"I've seen to it that you receive full credit for last year," Mr. Atkins continued seriously. "I know under normal circumstances you wouldn't have gotten into trouble. You've done excellent work here at school. I hope you'll put the past behind you and concentrate on what you can become." He pushed back his chair and stood up. "Roy, I want you back as student body director of activities and as president of the Youth Coordinating Council. I understand you're senior editor of the yearbook, too. I wish you well in your endeavors." He held out his hand. "Remember, you have my full support."

Roy stood up and grasped the extended hand. "I—I don't know what to say, sir," he stammered. "I won't disappoint you!"

"That's what I'm counting on."

Mr. Atkins' words were still fresh in Roy's mind when he met again with the Sinners. "No more heists or break-ins," Roy told the boys firmly. "From now on we stay on the right side of the law."

Roy received no arguments. The complexion of the gang had changed dramatically from the year before. Most of the former members—Mick, Tony, Eddie, Buckeye, Red—all had received stiff adult sentences. Since the remaining members were more interested in boozing it up and cavorting with the Saints than in stealing cars ("We'll save the town and ruin the girls," quipped one lusty Sinner), weekend sex parties took first place on the Sinners' agenda.

Sheila, leader of the Saints, was a tall redhead with a nice build and a certain worldly toughness about her. She hosted the parties in a large old house off South Street, warmly greeting the Sinners as they arrived sporting bottles of beer and gin.

There was always rock-and-roll music blaring—Elvis screaming "Jailhouse Rock" or Jerry Lee Lewis belting out "Whole Lotta Shakin' Going On." The Saints and the Sinners would dance a little, drink, and dance some more. Sometimes when the beer and gin took effect, the boys would dare Sheila to try something outlandish—drink a bottle of whiskey to see how much she could hold, or do a striptease dance on the table, or take on all the guys. Sheila never refused a challenge.

Eventually the lights would dim, and romantic ballads would replace the frenetic rock beat. While Johnny Mathis trilled "Chances Are" or Sam Cooke crooned "You Send Me," couples would drift off to the various corners of the house.

During his senior year, perhaps out of guilt or from loyalty to Mr. Atkins' high principles, Roy attempted to introduce the gang to some positive pursuits. "I don't see why we can't become a service club in the community," he told the guys one evening as they sat in their clubhouse over the Lookout Drive-in.

"Man, you been rubbin' elbows with too many principals and mayors," scoffed one greasy-haired youth.

"Yeah," drawled another. "What do we wanta help people for?"

"To build up our image," replied Roy. "It's simple. We can help people on the road who are having car trouble. Then we hand them a card that says 'Help Courtesy of the Sinners.' Before long people will start respecting us."

"I s'pose it can't hurt," scowled the first fellow. "So long as we don't have to give up our beer parties and poker runs."

During school hours, Roy tackled his responsibilities with his usual vigor, involving himself in many facets of Artesia High life: varsity football, the annual staff, the rally committee, school election, assemblies, and a dozen social activities. He even served as foreman of the student court jury which meted out punishment for offenses committed by Artesia students.

But Roy still wasn't satisfied. No matter how many accomplishments he chalked up, no matter how much fun he tried to have, he felt empty inside, inadequate. Was there no way to gain a sense of self-worth? What was life all about if a guy couldn't fill the emptiness?

One afternoon Roy sat eating his lunch on the senior square, a section of the campus reserved only for seniors, when someone sat down beside him. Roy glanced over and thought ruefully, *Oh, no, not Bill Page!* Bill was editor-in-chief of the yearbook, so he and Roy worked together closely on layouts and paste-ups, but outside of class Roy avoided Bill like the plague. Bill was a puzzle; he was what Roy would call a "real tough dude"—a short, solid Italian with a glint in his eye that said, *Don't mess with me.* But at the same time he had a reputation for being a religious fanatic. Several times he had invited Roy to church.

Roy had fallen into the habit of crossing the street or walking around a building to avoid Bill. He had even considered giving up his position as senior editor when he learned Bill would be editor-in-chief. But there were always times, like now, when he couldn't evade the runty crusader.

Bill was smiling. "You don't look so good today, Roy. Anything wrong?"

Roy scowled. "Man, I'm great. What could be wrong?"

Bill opened his lunch and removed a sandwich from wax paper. "Bologna again," he said. "What's yours?"

"Peanut butter." Roy took a generous bite, but it made a dry lump in his throat that was hard to swallow.

"That was something, huh," said Bill, "you and me tying for first place?"

"What?" said Roy.

"You know, the way we tied for selling the most advertising for the yearbook. The annual's making four-hundred bucks profit this year. Usually it runs a loss."

"Oh, yeah," Roy answered vaguely.

"You really don't look too happy," persisted Bill.

Silently Roy thought, *Who can be happy with Page around?* Aloud he answered, "So who cares?"

Bill shifted his position and looked Roy in the eye. "Maybe you don't know it, but God cares what happens to you. Why don't you give him a chance to help you with your problems?"

Roy stood up and crumpled his lunch sack with his fist. "Don't talk to me about that stuff. I tried religion and it doesn't work and I don't want to hear it!" He turned and stalked away.

Roy wasn't sure why Bill made him so angry. Maybe because people usually didn't come right out and talk so openly, so personally about God. Or maybe Roy was annoyed because it seemed like such a contradiction: a cool guy like Bill—top student and athlete, popular with the chicks, with one of the best custom cars on campus—talking about God like he was an old friend.

Long ago Roy had convinced himself that God belonged to little kids and old ladies, but now Bill was spoiling that smug stereotype. How could a hep guy get such a kick out of God? Page even belonged to a Christian car club—the Baptist Bolters. What did God and a car club have in common?

During the school year, whenever Roy had encountered Bill on campus, Bill had offered his usual cheerful greeting: "Remember, Roy, God loves you."

Even when Roy had retorted, "If you ever talk to me about God again, I'll break your head," Bill had smiled cunningly and replied, "OK, but he really does love you."

Occasionally in class, as they worked together on the school annual, discussing ideas for the senior section, Bill would suggest, "If you have some time this weekend, how about going to church with me?"

"No, thank you," Roy would answer briskly.

Bill would nod and say, "Well, you know God loves you."

It irritated Roy that one little guy could prompt such mixed feelings. He ridiculed Bill's religious fervor, but at the same time yearned to feel the peace and joy Bill knew. Deep inside Roy respected this pint-sized dynamo who obviously had something going for him.

One day toward the end of second semester Bill invited Roy to a church spaghetti dinner, adding with a sly grin, "There'll be lots of food and girls!"

Roy surprised even himself by replying, "OK, I'll go . . . I like to eat."

On the night of the dinner, Roy met Bill in front of the First Baptist Church of Lakewood, wearing his Sinners skull and crossbones jacket. He figured if he embarrassed Bill enough, Bill might not invite him back again. But the gesture was wasted. Bill eagerly introduced Roy to all his friends who, in turn, welcomed him like a long-lost brother. Roy had no way of knowing Bill's youth group had been praying for him for many months.

After the dinner, several teenagers stood up and talked about how knowing Christ personally gave them meaning and purpose in life. "Jesus filled the vacuum," one girl asserted, "and now I know what life is all about."

Roy found himself listening with unexpected hunger. The thought struck him, *If only I could have what these kids have!* But no. He wasn't like them, never could be. An impenetrable wall stood between them and him. The last thing on earth Roy wanted people to think was . . . *Comstock got religion!*

CHAPTER FIFTEEN

The first of June, 1958, two weeks before their high school graduation, Bill Page stopped Roy in the hall and said, "How would you like to go to the mountains with me this weekend?"

"It sounds great," said Roy, "but I'm supposed to ride in the Artesia parade with Governor Knight on Saturday afternoon."

"I could bring you back Saturday morning," suggested Bill.

Roy agreed to go—how often could he get a free trip to the mountains? It wasn't until Friday night, as they pulled into the campgrounds at Mount Palomar and Roy spotted young people carrying Bibles, that he learned the full story: Bill had brought him to the senior youth retreat of the First Baptist Church of Lakewood.

Man, I've been had! Roy told himself angrily. His first impulse was to take Bill's car and make his escape. But he didn't dare get into trouble again, so he joined the festivities, grudgingly.

· That evening the speaker, Wayne Hough, who was late in arriving, announced, "Because I'm so late, I'm not going to preach tonight."

Roy let out an involuntary "Whew!" At least he wouldn't have to sit through a sermon.

"But I want to tell you about a Friend of mine who is so wonderful I have to share him with you," continued Wayne. He began to talk about Jesus Christ.

Roy tried to close his mind, but something the man was saying caught his attention and held it.

"Young people, if you had been there when Christ stood before Pilate, beaten and spit upon, a crown of thorns pressing his brow, and if you had looked into his eyes, he would have said, 'I love you. I'm wearing these thorns for you.' And if you had been with Christ as he climbed the hill of Calvary and fell beneath the weight of his cross, he would have looked at you with tenderness and said, 'I love you. I'm carrying this cross for you.' "

Roy shifted restlessly in his seat. Bill must have told the preacher he was there. Why else would the man be talking directly to him?

The speaker's voice grew solemn. "If you had been there as they pounded the nails in Christ's hands and feet, and as they lifted the cross high and dropped it into the ground, leaving Christ hanging in anguish between heaven and earth, he would have looked down at you with eyes of compassion and said, 'I love you. I'm dying on the cross for you—because I love you.' "

The minister paused and gazed around at the silent faces. When he spoke again, his voice swelled with triumph. "If you had been there when Christ rose from the grave and later when he stood on Mount Olivet ready to ascend into heaven, he would have looked at you and said, 'I am going to prepare a place for you and I will come again to take you home forever—because I love you.' "

Suddenly Roy realized the man was giving an invitation. "If you want to accept Christ as Savior, won't you come forward and let me pray with you?" In those few moments Roy's heart began to beat furiously. So it was true after all, he marveled. Christ was real—and he loved Roy! Roy could hardly hear the speaker over the pounding in his chest. He wanted desperately to get up out of his seat and go. But another voice intruded: *You don't want these kids to think Comstock got religion, do you?*

Shutting out the opposing voices, Roy gripped his chair and forced himself to remain seated.

That night in his cabin Roy tossed and turned, unable to sleep. Over and over he heard the words, *I love you . . . I love you . . . I died for you . . . because I love you.*

Around five o'clock in the morning, he could take it no longer. He got up out of his bunk, dressed, and quietly stole out of his cabin. He hiked into the woods, driven by a torment as dark and impalpable as the night. He found a large tree, knelt beside it, and looked up into the heavens. "God, God, are you really there?" he cried, his voice jarring the stillness. "Can you really do for me what you've done for these other kids? If you can, forgive me and come into my life and let me be yours forever."

Roy knew in the moment he prayed that God did exactly what he'd said he would do. It was as if a thousand-pound weight had been lifted from his shoulders.

He jumped up in excitement. He had to tell someone. He decided the logical person to tell at five o'clock in the morning was the preacher. He ran back to camp, found Wayne Hough's cabin, and hammered vigorously on the door.

When the sleepy-eyed man answered, pulling his bathrobe around him, Roy blurted out, "I did it, I did it, I did it!"

The startled preacher cried, "What'd you do? Who'd you kill? What happened?"

"I let Jesus in my heart," declared Roy.

Wayne managed a surprised grin. "Come on in and tell me about it," he said.

In the hour that followed, Roy and the minister read together from God's Word. The verses from 1 John 5 and Romans 5 offered wonderful news to Roy. His salvation was based, not on how good he could be, but on what Christ had already done in shedding his blood on Calvary.

Before Roy left the preacher's cabin, he asked, "How do I know that my life will change, that I'll be any different?"

"Listen to this," suggested Wayne. He turned to 2 Corinthians 5:17 and read, "Therefore, if any man be in Christ, he is a new creature; old things are passed away; behold, all things are become new."

"That sounds good to me," said Roy.

Moments later Roy stood at the mountain's edge at sunrise, silently watching brilliant beams of gold wash the tops of the clouds. He could almost imagine Christ sitting on his throne in that dazzling early morning sky. Roy had fought God for a very long time, but now he was at peace. He was a member of God's family; for the first time in his life he really belonged.

Still later, during morning devotions, Wayne invited Roy to share his experience with the rest of the group. "Today I was supposed to be in a parade in Artesia with Governor Knight," he said with a grin. "Bill Page was going to drive me back early this morning. But something has happened to me that I have to tell you about. It was Bill who talked me into coming here. Page doesn't give up on a guy. I'm glad he didn't give up on me." He looked over at Bill and was surprised to see tears glistening in his eyes—tears and joy too. As Roy went on to relate his experience, he felt the sensation of "locking in" his decision to trust Christ. He had no doubt; his decision was real.

That afternoon, riding back down the mountain with Bill, Roy wondered how he was going to tell the gang about his decision to follow Christ. They would be having their usual drinking party next Friday night, and they would expect him to be there. What was he going to do?

As Friday night approached, Roy decided to attend the Saints and Sinners' party. Maybe no one would notice the difference in him; in fact, maybe there was no difference. The Bible said he was a new creature. Was he really? Or did he just imagine the change?

When Roy arrived at the party on Friday evening, Sheila welcomed him with a kiss and a drink. The Saints and Sinners were dancing energetically to a strident Chuck Berry disc. Roy mingled for a while, offering brief greetings and making small talk with the guys. Then he noticed he hadn't touched his drink. He didn't even want it.

He gazed self-consciously around the room and realized with a start that he felt as out of place here as he had felt the first time he went to church with Bill. *I don't belong here*, he marveled silently. *I've made a decision to follow God.*

Roy's thoughts were interrupted by a fellow Sinner who nudged his arm and said, "Hey, Comstock, drink up!"

Roy stared absently at the drink in his hand. "What? Oh, hi, Joe. I—I don't think I want this after all." He set the glass on the table. "Actually, I've got to be going."

"Going?" echoed Joe. "The party's just getting started. You'll miss all the fun."

Another Sinner joined them. "Somebody mention fun?"

"Comstock's cuttin' out," replied Joe.

"You got something better going somewhere else?" quizzed the other youth.

"No," said Roy. He thought a moment, then added, "Or

maybe I do. Last weekend I made a decision to—to let Christ into my life. I wasn't sure what difference he would make, but—well, I see now I can't keep up this drinking. I'm going to leave."

"You're kiddin', aren't you, man?" came the quick reply.

"You're gonna have us thinkin' you're a religious fanatic or something," added Joe.

"Think what you want," said Roy. "I'm leaving the gang."

Joe's expression fell. "Hey, you mean it, don'tcha! What'll we tell the other guys?"

"I don't care," said Roy. "Tell them I got religion—no, wait, tell them I got *Christ*. Besides, I'll probably be going into the Army Reserves after graduation next week, so I won't be around anyway."

"You'll be back," said Joe, following Roy to the door. "It won't last. It's just a phase. You get religion; then after a few months you find out there's nothin' to it. Wait and see. You'll be back!"

Roy gazed momentarily at Joe. "No, I won't. Not this time," he answered. He walked out the door and made it a point not to look back.

CHAPTER SIXTEEN

Two weeks after Roy graduated from high school he entered the Army Reserves. For basic training he went to Fort Ord, near San Francisco. There he had his first real opportunity to practice his new faith. Never one to do anything half-heartedly, Roy spoke out vigorously, unashamedly for Christ. Every morning he knelt by his bunk, prayed, and read his Bible, oblivious to the curious stares of the fifty other men sharing his barracks.

Almost immediately Roy was tagged *deacon, chaplain,* or *preacher.* But he didn't mind the guys making fun of him. He was a new Christian and he liked being a Christian. There was an exhilaration, an immense satisfaction in obeying God and telling others about Jesus. Nothing else in life had given him such peace and joy.

During Roy's stay at Fort Ord he spent his weekends with his brother Milt in San Francisco. Milt, still in the Navy, also tended bar and worked as a bouncer in a nightclub. He lived on Nob Hill with his second wife Ida. He drove a Lincoln Continental and wore the finest clothes. Roy was thrilled at the opportunity to get reacquainted with his oldest brother, his childhood hero. He was impressed by Milt's style and class.

Milt, still the family protector, gave Roy clothes and helped him purchase an old 1941 Pontiac. As the weeks passed, a close relationship developed between the two brothers. Although Roy couldn't bring himself to witness directly to Milt, he was careful to uphold his new standards, and both brothers recognized that somehow Roy was a different person.

After basic training, Roy was transferred from Fort Ord to Camp Irwin near Death Valley. His MOS (Military Occupational Specialty) was "light wheel vehicle mechanic," but he spent most of his time driving and working on tanks. Roy, who had spent the last six years seeking diversions to keep him away from home, now gladly made the long drive each weekend to his folks' little house behind the Morrisons. Roy enjoyed going home. And he looked forward to the fellowship with his friends at First Baptist Church of Lakewood. He wasn't running anymore.

Over the months he had noticed a change in his feelings; he no longer hated his mother. The bitterness was gone. Often now he looked at Bertha Comstock as if seeing her for the first time; he was beginning to understand how much he had tortured this frail woman with his hatred, and now he asked God to forgive him.

As Roy studied the Scriptures, he did a great deal of thinking about his relationship with God and with his mother. He mulled over what had happened in his life, the miracle of it all. He realized that a holy God had looked down on his sinful heart and had every right to toss him aside as worthless. "But God chose to redeem me anyway," he marveled aloud. "He selected me, Roy Comstock, head of the Sinners, to be a member of his family. So how can I condemn and reject my mother?" His prayer became, "Help me, God, to love her as you love me."

In December 1958, Roy completed his six-month tour of duty in the Army Reserves and returned home. Within the next year he jumped from one job to another—from the assembly line of O'Keefe and Merritt in Los Angeles to an accordion studio in Bellflower, selling music lessons, to Stores Protective Association, where he worked as an investigator. His first assignment there was to become a shoe salesman at the May Company, in order to track down the culprit who was selling shoes "out the back door." Roy broke open the case when he discovered the manager peddling shoes to his friends and pocketing the cash.

The year was also a special time of growth for Roy. He enrolled at Cerritos College, attended discipleship classes led by Rod Toews at Lakewood, joined a gospel team, and took part in a jail ministry which provided an opportunity to share his testimony with those experiencing the same trauma of imprisonment he had faced. One Sunday he was invited to speak to 600 teenagers at Juvenile Hall in Los Angeles, where he himself had been confined just two short years before. When he had finished speaking, 213 boys professed a desire to trust Christ.

As Roy became increasingly involved in witnessing, he developed a real burden for evangelism. Perhaps God wanted him to have a ministry among juveniles. Or maybe the Lord wanted him to be a preacher. That's what the young people at church kept telling him, but Roy wasn't sure what God had in mind.

During the summer of 1960, Roy began to feel a strong need for additional training. Lakewood pastor Harold Carlson, a warm, outgoing, positive man, encouraged Roy to attend Bethel College in St. Paul, Minnesota. "You're already a good speaker," he told Roy, "but with professional training there's no telling how God will be able to use you."

That fall Roy began attending Bethel College. To pay his way he worked at a Montgomery Ward store selling ladies' shoes, but his meager income wouldn't stretch far enough. Roy figured if God wanted him at Bethel, he would provide the additional funds. And God did. Often when Roy opened his mailbox he found sums of money from friends on campus or, more often, anonymous gifts.

While at Bethel, Roy met several students who would prove to be lifelong friends: his roommate, Ken Mulder, who would one day serve as best man in his wedding; Darrell Johnson, who, years later, would work closely with Roy in evangelism; and Bob Hart, who would establish the American Evangelism Association, a ministry with which Roy would serve as evangelist.

Roy returned home from Bethel over the Christmas holidays for one of the most unexpected and rewarding experiences of his life. On New Year's Eve the young people of First Baptist, Lakewood, gathered in the sanctuary for their customary watchnight service. Roy left the festivities momentarily to make a phone call in the pastor's study.

Suddenly a small, muscular stranger stepped inside and glared at Roy, his gnarled face strained with emotion. Roy replaced the

telephone receiver and offered a tentative smile. "Hello."
The man, clearly agitated, glanced around furtively. "I—I was
driving by and I saw the lights on. I heard—people singing."
"We're having our New Year's Eve service," said Roy. He
introduced himself and extended his hand, but the stranger
ignored it.
"Where's the preacher? Isn't this his office?"
"Yes," said Roy, "but he's not here now. Can I help you?"
"You can call me Jack if you want. It's not my name, but it's
better you don't know who I am."
"I don't understand," said Roy.
"Why should you understand?" returned the stranger. His
eyes narrowed ominously. "You know anything about—what
would you call it?—the syndicate? Organized crime? The
underworld? You ever hear of Mickey Cohen?"
Roy nodded. "Sure."
"Well, I'm second in command under Mickey. Only I could be
first. I could be right there on top giving the orders." The man's
face glistened with a strange intensity. "I drove around all
evening thinking about it. I got everything set up. But I couldn't
make up my mind. I drove around thinking, him or me? I kill him
or I kill myself. Or if I kill him maybe it's the same as killing me."
Roy stared hard at the curious visitor. "You—can't be
serious."
In a swift, startling gesture the man yanked the telephone off
the desk. "All I gotta do is make a call and I can have Mickey
Cohen snuffed out like that. Then I'd be the big boss!"
Roy's heart pounded like a mallet. "I—I know what it's like
being leader of a gang," he said. "But it's no good. It can't give
you peace."
The man looked imploringly at Roy. "Peace? You talk about
peace? You gotta be dead to have peace. You don't know the
pressures I'm under." He ran his fingers distractedly through his
hair. "My wife—she left me—took our kids away—said I'm not
fit. I got men breathing down my neck waiting for me to make a
wrong move. One way or the other, I want out!"
"Listen, Jack," said Roy, "I'd really like to help if you'd let me."
The wiry gangster eyed Roy suspiciously. "I don't even know
why I'm here. I saw the lights. It was like something drew me."
"You know what I think, Jack?" said Roy. "I think God

brought you here. I think he wants you to hear my story. You
see, I used to be like you. I felt the same bitterness and
frustration you feel."

The deep lines in the man's face settled into a rueful smile. He
rubbed his chin thoughtfully. "OK, so what's your story?"

The two sat down and Roy spent the next half hour sharing
what God had done in his life. He told Jack how he, too, could
accept Christ. When Roy paused, the man said, "My wife's a
Christian like you. She's prayed for me for years."

"I'd like to pray for you too," said Roy. He bowed his head
before Jack could protest. "Please, God, help Jack see that
you're his answer. Help him to accept your love." When Roy
opened his eyes he saw a broken expression on the man's face.

"Can those young people out there pray like you do?" he
asked.

"Sure they can," said Roy.

"All right, go get them and have them come in here and pray."

Roy summoned nearly a dozen friends from the sanctuary and
briefly explained the peculiar situation. "Let's just join hands right
now and pray for Jack," he concluded.

The young people, holding hands, formed a circle that
included the stranger. One by one the teenagers prayed. After a
few minutes there was a convulsive sob. The tormented man
collapsed on the floor and wept uncontrollably. Then he shouted,
"God, come into my life. Help me! Let me have Christ!"

When finally the man stood up, they all knew—they remarked
about it later—that he had changed. A warm glow eased his
calloused expression; a peacefulness replaced the desperation.
As midnight approached, Roy prayed with Jack again as he
sealed his decision to trust Christ. Then the man left as quickly,
as mysteriously, as he had arrived.

Over the next couple years Roy would often wonder about
the fate of this top gangland figure who had professed Christ on
New Year's Eve. Three years would pass before the two would
unexpectedly meet again and Roy would learn the astonishing
news: Jack, having reunited with his wife and children, was now
a highly respected evangelist faithfully serving the Lord.

After the holidays, still rejoicing over Jack's conversion, Roy
returned to Bethel College and completed his first semester. But
there was no way he could keep up the pace—working full time,

carrying a full class load, and squeezing in weekend evangelism. To complicate matters, Roy became ill with several abscessed teeth, missed two weeks of classes, and found himself with a mounting dental bill. He had a feeling God was trying to tell him something. It was time to move on.

In February 1961, Roy returned to California. In response to a newspaper ad, he went to work for Hall Industries, selling Rainbow vacuum cleaners. Because he no longer had his own car he had to borrow his dad's truck to make his calls; in fact, he was so broke he had to borrow gas money as well. And he had little to wear because his clothes, selected for Minnesota winters, were much too warm for the California sun.

In spite of the obstacles, Roy tackled his new job with his usual vigor and enthusiasm. He considered himself a pretty good salesman, so selling vacuum cleaners to housewives didn't look too difficult. But during his first month he made thirty-nine presentations and never sold a thing!

When he came home at night his dad would say, "Why don't you get a regular job? I can't afford this one." As the weeks passed, his father's protests grew more vehement: "What is this? You go away to college and you come back and sell vacuum cleaners. But no! Not even one sale yet. Can't you do something better than this?"

Roy had no answer. He was a flop at sales, but he didn't know why. Then one significant day he found out what was wrong. A lady telephoned the office and Gary Hall, the owner's son, took the call. A minute later Gary approached Roy and said, "That lady on the phone said the nicest young man was just out there showing her our machine."

"Oh, yeah," said Roy. "That was me."

"Well, now she wants to know how she can get one!" bellowed Gary. "Didn't it occur to you to tell her?"

So that was it. Roy hadn't attempted to close a deal! Gary Hall spent the next few days teaching Roy how to sell.

In the next two months Roy broke the company's records, sometimes selling as many as six vacuum cleaners a day. After three months on the job he was given his own office in Lynwood and was labeled Rainbow's "ninety-day wonder." Roy thrived on his success as a salesman. In fact, he began to spend his money even faster than he earned it. On his twenty-second birthday he went out and bought a new Cadillac convertible.

The more preoccupied Roy became with his business success, the farther behind lagged his spiritual growth. He stopped attending discipleship classes and no longer participated in a gospel team or the jail ministry; he rarely read his Bible or prayed anymore. He began to feel an emptiness creeping back into his life. To make matters worse, he suddenly found himself deep in debt; his Cadillac was repossessed; things were falling apart around him.

When Roy shared his problems with Rod Toews at Lakewood, Rod helped him to see that he was allowing other things to interfere with his relationship with Christ. Rod pointed out that God had to come first, above money or success. That day Roy renewed his commitment, yielding himself for God's service, whatever it might be.

Early in 1962, buoyed by a new zeal to serve the Lord, Roy joined a dozen young men from Lakewood who were organizing a gospel team. Shortly after joining the team, an incident once again raised the question for Roy: Should he enter the ministry? On a Sunday evening, the team drove down to San Diego to speak in a small Baptist church on Coronado Island. They received a tremendous response, with a number of people finding Christ as Savior.

After the service, the team's three-car caravan pushed through murky fog toward the ferry that would take them off the island. Suddenly, as they neared the ferry, Roy's 1956 Oldsmobile stopped dead. All the young men piled out of their cars and swarmed around Roy's stalled vehicle.

"I can't figure out what's wrong," he told them. "The engine's absolutely dead."

A little red-headed fellow spoke up, "Well, praise the Lord. He must want us to do something here."

Someone else said, "Hey, there's a place to eat over there. Let's go in and maybe the car will start when we come back."

Everyone agreed. They were starved!

Entering the dimly lit restaurant, they realized it was also a bar. "Well, this is the only place open and we're stuck here," said Roy. "Might as well make the best of it."

When the hostess came to seat them, Roy asked for a table away from the bar. She led them to a small private room where they were all able to sit at one table. While they waited for their food, they could hear the baritone singer in the next room belting out a popular song.

"Hey, wouldn't it be neat if we could sing *our* kind of music here?" said one of the guys.

"Why can't we?" said someone else.

A third youth responded, "OK, I'll get my trombone and music."

"And I'll get my trumpet," added a fourth fellow.

Minutes later the team's quartet stood beside their table singing gospel songs. It didn't take long for the manager, a squat little Jewish lady, to bustle in and snap angrily, "You can't do that in here!"

One of the team members rose to his full seven feet and placed his hand lightly on her shoulder. "Would you please come over here and let me talk to you about this?" he asked.

He took her over to one corner and witnessed briefly about Christ. After that she let them sing.

Shortly, the baritone from the other room came in and stood behind the quartet looking at the music. "I don't know these words," he said, "but let me sing with you guys. You sound pretty good."

They sang together for a while; then one of the team members began talking to the vocalist about Jesus. He led him to the Lord right there at the table.

Meanwhile Roy and Ron, the manager of the gospel team, sat chatting at the other end of the table. When the waiter came over to refill their water glasses, they both spoke at once: "Whosoever drinketh of this water shall thirst again; but whosoever drinketh of the water that I shall give him shall never thirst."

The waiter looked puzzled. "What are you guys talking about?"

Roy and Ron exchanged sly grins. Here was their cue. They shared their testimony. Moments later the man knelt between them at the table and asked Christ into his life. Before long other customers gathered curiously around the gospel team, listening to their music and asking questions about their faith. Before the team left the restaurant that night, nine people prayed to receive Christ as Savior.

When Roy returned to his car, he fully expected it to start. It didn't. He looked over at Ron and sighed, "Now what? Any ideas how we can get off this island?"

One of the guys spoke up from the back seat. "Well, we're close to the ferry. You see those two attendants in the booth over there? Maybe that's why we're still here."

"Let's find out," said Ron, opening the car door.

He and the other team member went over and talked with the two men. When they returned a little later, Ron was grinning jubilantly. "They both accepted Christ!" he exclaimed.

Amid cheers and praises, Roy tried the ignition again. The engine turned over and purred smoothly.

CHAPTER SEVENTEEN

On a warm Sunday in April, 1962, Roy joined his friend Roscoe Williams, Youth for Christ director, for an afternoon at the beach. They swam for a while, played a little volleyball, then sat down on the sand to catch their breath.

"How come we don't do this more often?" panted Roscoe, tossing Roy a towel.

"Too busy," returned Roy, stretching out on his back on the hot sand. He tucked the towel under his head and released the tension in his muscles to the pervasive warmth around him.

"I haven't seen you lately," remarked Roscoe lightly, "but I hear you're really cleaning up with your vacuum sales."

Roy chuckled, but kept his eyes closed against the blinding sun's rays. "The job's great—but my wallet's empty," he joked lamely. "I really got myself in debt. I gotta look up to see bottom."

"How'd you do that?"

"Easy. If I earned a thousand bucks, I spent fifteen hundred. You remember the Cadillac convertible I bought a while back?"

"Yeah. So where is it now?"

"They repossessed it," said Roy. "Here I was trying to show my dad that a Comstock finally had it made. All I showed him is how a fool blows his wad."

"Maybe you're spending too much on girls," suggested Roscoe with a grin. "I hear you're quite a ladies' man at Lakewood Baptist."

Roy smiled slyly. "Let's just say I believe in playing the field."

"Remind me not to invite you to North Long Beach Brethren."

"You already did," Roy chuckled. "Tonight."

"Oh, yeah. So I did." Roscoe sat forward and circled his knees with his arms. "Roy, you're what—twenty-three? You ever think about settling down—getting married?"

Roy leaned up on one elbow and peered squint-eyed at his friend. "Funny you should ask that."

"How so? You making plans I don't know about?"

Roy grinned broadly. "Yeah. Plans to stay a bachelor!"

"You sound like you really mean it," said Roscoe.

"I do," replied Roy. "I like my freedom. I figure I can do more for the Lord if I'm not tied down. Besides, my family has a pretty poor track record in marriage."

"That doesn't mean it has to be that way for you."

Roy sat up and gazed thoughtfully toward the ocean. "I don't know. Maybe I'm afraid to have a permanent relationship with a woman," he said huskily. "I'm not sure I could provide for her. I'd rather not have a family at all than have them go through what I did as a kid."

Roscoe nodded sympathetically. They were both silent for a minute; then Roscoe gave Roy an unexpected nudge. "Speaking of women, I just spotted someone you've got to meet."

Roy looked around. Two girls in bathing suits were approaching.

Roscoe stood up and waved. "Wanda's the gal I've been dating lately," he told Roy. "The other girl's her best friend— Judy. Just for the record, you can take Judy out if you want to, but Wanda's mine."

"Thanks a lot," grinned Roy, standing up and brushing off patches of clinging sand.

Roscoe greeted the girls and made brief introductions. Roy gazed at the trim young woman in the purple two-piece bathing suit. Her skin was a golden brown, a glistening mixture of sun, sea, and sand; and her blonde hair was windblown, matted with salt spray against the back of her neck. "Looks like you've been here all day," he said.

She smiled. "Just about." Gingerly she touched her shoulder. "We're absolutely cremated, aren't we, Judy?"

"Maybe a good swim would cool us all off," suggested Roscoe, taking Wanda's hand.

The four of them ran laughing into the ocean and played like children in the waves, splashing one another, chasing the tide. Roy, in his exuberance, picked Wanda up in his arms, lifted her high, and tossed her into the water. She screamed as his fingers pressed painfully into her tender, sunburned skin. Choking and sputtering as she came up out of the spumy salt water, she wiped her eyes and glared at Roy. "You clod! You almost killed me!" She turned and stalked out of the water.

Roy followed her, floundering against the convulsive whitecaps. "Wait, Wanda. What's wrong?"

Wanda, reaching the shore and regaining her composure, replied, "Nothing. I'm all right. But we've got to be going. Judy— she's a beautician, and she's going to do my hair before church tonight. See you around, Roy."

Roscoe walked the girls to their car, then returned. "What did you think of Wanda?" he asked.

Roy shrugged. "Let's just say neither of us made much of an impression."

But when Roy saw Wanda at church that evening, he changed his opinion. Wanda looked gorgeous. Her face glowed; she wore a lovely, form-flattering dress; her blonde hair was attractively styled.

"I almost didn't recognize you," he told her approvingly.

"I wouldn't have known you either," she admitted. "I guess we all looked pretty scroungy today."

Roscoe interrupted with, "Where's Judy? She's supposed to be Roy's date tonight."

"She couldn't make it after all," said Wanda quickly.

"That's OK," said Roy. "I just spotted someone I know."

He left momentarily, and Roscoe demanded, "What's going on here?"

Wanda shrugged her shoulders helplessly. "Judy wouldn't go out with him. He was such a creep at the beach, so overbearing and outrageous—"

Wanda changed the subject abruptly when Roy returned, smiling, leading a young lady by the hand. "This is Charlotte," he said. "She'll be joining us."

After church, the foursome drove over to the Park Pantry Restaurant. There they were escorted to a booth and Roy found himself sitting across from Wanda. Somehow he didn't notice anyone else for the rest of the evening. They chatted briefly; then he realized he didn't know her last name.

"Let's see," he said, trying to sound casual, "You're Wanda—?"

"Schimming. Wanda Schimming."

He liked the way she smiled when she said her name. But he would never remember Schimming to save his life. And he certainly couldn't be obvious and write it down while Roscoe was sitting there. Silently he told himself, *Schimming, Schimming, Schimming.* He created mental images: a shimmy in a wheel, the way a car shimmied, a girl shimmying.

"So where do you work, Wanda Schimming?" he asked.

"California Chassis," she replied brightly.

Boy, she's got a nice chassis herself, he mused.

"I'm their receptionist and biller," she added.

"Tell me about it," suggested Roy. They talked all evening. Later, neither would recall what Charlotte or Roscoe did or said. Roy could think only of Wanda, so friendly and lively, fun to be with.

The following Sunday night Roy returned to Wanda's church. He knew she would be there. As he expected, she was with Roscoe. After the service, a group of young people drove over to the Park Pantry for dessert. Roy made it a point to sit next to Wanda. Somehow he had to get her attention. He started telling dumb jokes, saying things that made no sense, acting silly. Surprisingly, she laughed; she was actually amused by his stupid prattling.

During the following week Roy managed to get Wanda's number from a friend. Squelching a rare nervousness, he telephoned and said, "Would you go out with me Saturday night? I'm speaking at a Youth for Christ meeting, but I thought we could have dinner together first."

"That sounds like a plan," she replied cheerfully.

They went to the Sierra Restaurant and had the seafood platter. Roy wore his black mohair suit and a white tie. Wanda, her hair backcombed in an attractive flip, looked fantastic in a long, melon-colored chiffon dress.

When they arrived at the youth meeting, Roscoe, who was already leading the singing, spotted them coming down the aisle and glowered indignantly until they took their seats near the front. Roy shifted uneasily, feeling a bit like a traitor. But then again, why should he feel guilty? Wanda had made it clear she wasn't Roscoe's girl.

Although Wanda was nearly nineteen, her parents still expected her to be home by ten. Roy walked her to her door and was careful not to kiss her good night. Since becoming a Christian, he had heard it wasn't proper to kiss a girl on the first date. But on their second date several days later, he did kiss her—quickly, without warning, just as she turned to go through the door.

In the next two weeks Roy and Wanda saw each other frequently. Since she worked only a few blocks from his Lynwood office, she dropped by to visit him when he worked evenings. Sometimes, after work, they would sit and chat in Roy's car in the parking lot behind his office. There in the cozy, dim quietness of the automobile, Wanda, usually reticent and shy, found it surprisingly easy to talk and share her life. Roy seemed to know intuitively how to draw her out of herself.

"What were you like as a little kid?" he asked one evening.

She smiled, remembering. "I had a good childhood . . . not at all eventful like yours. I've spent my whole life on East Sixty-fourth Street in Long Beach. The elementary school was across the street; junior high was seven blocks away; high school, four blocks. So there was about a mile I considered my territory. While I was growing up, my dad was a truck driver, gone a lot. My mother's always been a housewife. We've just lived a very peaceful life—my folks, my older brother Howard, and I."

Roy gazed quizzically at her. "So that's it? No problems, no traumas? A smooth, perfect existence?"

Wanda returned his gaze. "Does it sound too easy, too perfect?"

Roy gently rubbed her shoulder. "Yeah, it does a little. Maybe I just feel that way because of the hell I went through as a kid."

Wanda's expression tensed slightly. "My parents were always very strict. Overprotective, I suppose. I guess my greatest fear was of not living up to the standards they set for me." She forced a smile. "But I guess it worked out all right. They always called me their good little girl."

"And were you?"

Wanda looked surprised. "Yes, of course. If I didn't agree with what they said, I kept my feelings to myself. My brother—he rebelled, so he was always being punished. I saw what happened to him, and I knew I couldn't risk my folks' disapproval. I would have pleased them if it killed me. I couldn't bear to disappoint them."

Roy grinned. "You sound too good to be true."

Wanda let out an involuntary laugh. "I hope not. I'm just me— a basically optimistic, agreeable, uncomplicated person."

Roy ran his finger lightly over her chin. "I wish I had known you when you were little. I bet you were a cute little girl."

She laughed again. "Oh, was I competitive! I liked school and got good grades, but I wouldn't try anything unless I was sure I could do well at it. I was pretty good at sports, too. In the summer we'd play 'kick the can' and 'red light, green light'—all that good stuff. And I loved roller skating and bowling and swimming. Even baseball. I guess I was quite a tomboy."

"Tell me, when did you become a Christian?" asked Roy.

"During my senior year of high school—at a Youth for Christ meeting. Then I got involved in all the church activities; it was great. It helped me overcome some of my shyness."

"You don't seem so shy to me," remarked Roy.

She smiled faintly. "I guess I'm not—with you."

Roy drew her close. "You know what you are? Special. I don't think I've ever met anyone as special as you."

The following Sunday night Roy and Wanda attended church at First Baptist, Lakewood. Roy was unusually quiet this evening; he knew Wanda had noticed, but he couldn't confide in her yet. Old anxieties were resurfacing—his fear of becoming too involved, of taking on responsibilities he couldn't handle. Ultimately he was afraid to admit he was in love; he had never been in love before. It would change everything—the direction of his life, all his plans. Yet he wanted desperately for Wanda to love him.

Sitting beside her in the pew, Roy was too preoccupied even to join in singing the familiar hymns—until a phrase from one song disarmed him completely: *"We love Him because He first loved us."* At that moment a thought struck Roy suddenly. How can I expect Wanda to love me if I'm not willing to admit that *I* love *her?*

After the service, as they sat in his car in the church parking lot, Roy said, "Honey, there's something I want to talk to you about. I know we've known each other for only a month, but I don't want to go with anyone else. Only you."

"I feel that way too," she said softly.

He tilted her chin toward him. "I love you, Wanda."

She caught her breath and murmured, "I love you too."

"Then it's settled," he said. He felt elated, excited. He felt like shouting. He embraced her hard, laughing. "Honey, we're going steady!"

CHAPTER EIGHTEEN

On June 13, 1962, nearly two months from the day they had met, Roy and Wanda were sitting in his car in front of her house after a date, discussing their dreams for the future—how many children they wanted, what their names would be, where they hoped to live, the kind of furniture they liked.

Wanda's mother flipped the porch light switch to signal that it was time to come in, when Wanda asked, "How come we're talking about all these things, anyway?"

Roy struggled for the right words. "Well, because I figure someday we'll . . . you know."

"No, I don't know," said Wanda. "You've never asked me."

Roy stared out the car window, drumming his fingers nervously on the steering wheel. "Well, we know we're in love, even though we haven't been going together very long." His voice fell to scarcely a whisper. "I'd like you to marry me."

"What did you say?" Wanda asked quickly.

He looked at her and repeated, "I'd like you to marry me, Wanda."

She went into his arms. "Oh, yes, Roy, I'll marry you."

For a long moment he held her close. She was soft and warm and smelled deliciously of perfume. Roy marveled over his good fortune—at last to have someone to love, someone so dear and good and gentle.

Later that week they purchased her rings at a local jewelry

store where Roy opened an account; but since he was still deeply in debt, it was Wanda who made the monthly payments.

Wanda's parents, Mary and Leo Schimming, were not pleased with the engagement. They had never liked—or trusted— salesmen. Their philosophy was that if a salesman ever got his foot in the door, you should slam it. They gave their permission for the engagement but adopted a skeptical wait-and-see attitude toward the impending marriage.

Roy's parents, on the other hand, were vocally enthusiastic. Howard gave Wanda a big bear hug and boomed, "Roy, you really got yourself a diamond!" Bertha added in a soft, pleased voice, "You've got a fine girl there, son. Take good care of her."

But in a hapless effort to bridge the gap between the two families, Bertha Comstock only managed to underscore their differences. Halfway through a wedding shower, to which she invited Wanda's family and friends, Bertha interrupted the festivities to introduce a lady who sold houseware products. The woman stood up and proceeded to give her sales demonstration to the group of stunned ladies. It was a funny but embarrassing situation, and an evening Wanda would never forget.

Wanda, who always felt ill at ease meeting people, found it particularly hard to relate to Roy's family. Because most of them were such large people, she had the feeling they eyed her and thought, Oh, my, she needs to put on some weight! And coming from a home that was spotlessly clean, Wanda was disturbed by the muss and clutter of the small Comstock house. Wanda found the Comstocks openly demonstrative too—a distressing fact, since she had been raised with little outward show of affection.

She tried to tell Roy of her reaction. "Your father—he scares me—he's so big and gruff, so overpowering. And is everyone in your family so huggy-huggy, kissy-kissy?"

"Afraid so," Roy chuckled in amusement. Pulling her into his arms, he murmured, "What's so bad about being huggy-huggy, kissy-kissy?"

He held her firmly, possessively in his embrace until gradually she relaxed against him.

"It's not so bad after all," she murmured softly, but her words were cut off by his lips.

The engagement required adjustments from both Roy and

Wanda, but Roy was still fighting a private inner war that went beyond his newfound happiness. Should he remain in business, where financial success was almost guaranteed—or should he enter professional evangelism, which offered little financial security? When he shared his dilemma with Wanda, she was more than supportive; she shared his vision to serve Christ, and encouraged him to step out in faith wherever God led. In fact, it was Roy's very zeal for God, his daring and independence, that had first excited her imagination. She loved him for his courage, his desire to stand up and be counted, to act on his conviction, to step out and conquer the world for Christ.

So shortly after their engagement they made a decision: Roy would quit his job with the Rainbow Company and go into full-time evangelistic work. Associating himself with youth evangelist Louie Rhoden and the Christian Workers Service Bureau, Roy began holding youth meetings, counseling with teenagers, and teaching classes in dating, courtship, and marriage.

He discovered soon enough that *teaching* ideal principles was easier than *living* them. One guideline he taught was that a couple should be engaged a full year before marrying. He gradually eliminated that theory as he and Wanda moved their wedding date up from one year to eleven months and eventually to seven months. Teaching placed a greater responsibility on him in other ways, too. One day he was a bit disconcerted when Wanda's father, learning Roy was teaching a class in Christian courtship, inquired, "Do you practice what you teach?" Roy coughed nervously and replied, "Yes, sir!"

Roy and Wanda's seven-month engagement was basically a happy, busy time for both of them. Wanda continued to work. She joined Roy for his meetings whenever possible. The only shadow over their joy was a persistent lack of money, but they were too blissfully in love to consider finances a serious problem. Only as their wedding date approached did Roy admit he needed a steady income. In December, after five months with Louie Rhoden, Roy left evangelism to work for Penn Mutual Life Insurance Company in Long Beach. But he wasn't happy with his new position; the company stressed making sales pitches to friends and relatives, and taught that there were only two kinds of people in the world: the ones *you* know and the ones *they* know.

While Roy peddled insurance, exhausting his list of family members and acquaintances and struggling vainly to show a profit, Wanda willingly assumed responsibility for their financial obligations. She paid for their entire wedding and also chopped away at some of Roy's long-standing debts. But even her income wouldn't cover everything. She had to borrow money from her father for the wedding invitations and ninety dollars from her grandmother for the first month's rent on a furnished one-bed-room apartment in Bixby Knolls.

Roy and Wanda were married on January 25, 1963, in the First Baptist Church of Lakewood. Pastor Harold Carlson performed the ceremony; Herman Hosier, from the Haven of Rest quartet, sang. Ken Mulder, Roy's buddy from Bethel, stood with him as best man. Wanda's friend Judy Nickerson was maid of honor. Nearly 300 people attended.

As Roy stood nervously watching Wanda come down the aisle toward him, he thought, *I don't want to disappoint her. I don't want to let her down. Please, God, let me be good enough for her.*

There was no money for a honeymoon, so after the wedding Roy and Wanda went with Ken and Sharon Mulder to the Park Pantry for coffee. The newlyweds spent their wedding night in their tiny Bixby Knolls apartment.

Some time after the wedding Roy met his friend Roscoe Williams for coffee. The two chatted for a while; then Roscoe said, "Did you ever wonder if maybe you had the wrong girl?"

"Never," said Roy, "but sometimes I've wondered if I was the wrong guy."

Roscoe nodded, tight-lipped, and replied, "Yeah, so have I."

This wasn't the last time someone would question whether Wanda had made a wise choice in marrying Roy.

CHAPTER NINETEEN

Full-time evangelism beckoned Roy again. In June 1963, he accepted a summer position as youth director for a small church in Los Alamitos. Then, in September he and Wanda moved to Whittier and Roy began attending Biola College. To help pay his way, he became custodian and part-time youth director for the Greenleaf Avenue Baptist Church in Whittier, and Wanda returned to secretarial work.

Roy also became involved again with the Christian Jail Workers. He served as juvenile chaplain for the Los Angeles County Probation Department and was one of the first to participate in the in-camp chaplain program for the county. He spent each weekend away from home counseling boys and holding Bible studies and Sunday school services at Camp Five in San Dimas, the very facility where he himself had served time as a juvenile offender.

As chaplain, Roy had free run of the camp. He spent time talking with guys in the barracks or playing basketball or Ping-Pong with them in the recreation room. He openly shared his own background, the fact that he had served time here just as they were doing now. "This used to be my bunk," he would remark, or, "I used to eat here," or, "I worked in this very spot."

The boys were impressed and responsive. Roy had straightened out his life, so maybe they could do the same. Over the months Roy saw many of the boys accept Christ as their Savior.

Roy would remember one boy in particular—a husky, good-looking black boy, a former heroin addict who had just come through withdrawal. Roy spent a great deal of time with that boy and saw him respond to Christ. When it came time for the youth to return home, Roy, knowing the problems the teenager would face on the outside, wanted to give him something special to remember him by. He handed him his own well-worn, underlined Bible. With an appreciative grin, the youth promised to keep it and read it.

The week before Roy and Wanda's first wedding anniversary, Roy made a special announcement to the boys in his Bible study at Camp Five. "Next week I've got a surprise," he said. "I'm going to bring my wife along and we're going to celebrate our anniversary with you guys—because this is where I want to be on this exciting anniversary."

The boys cheered loudly, and the following week, when Roy walked in with Wanda, their cheers were accented with exclamations of "oooh" and "aaah" and "wow!" Wanda was nervous about facing the roomful of juveniles; she hadn't planned to spend her first anniversary in such an unorthodox manner. But Roy's enthusiasm was contagious, and now she nodded brightly and smiled and passed out pieces of wedding cake saved from the year before. No one seemed to mind that the cake was a bit icy, not having been thawed out completely.

The group sang a few rousing choruses; then Roy stood up and told the boys, "You notice I have a beautiful wife, and my life is really turned around from a few years ago when I sat where you're sitting now. Wanda and I are here now because we love you. We want you to know God loves you, too. Christ changed my life. He can change yours if you'll let him."

The boys responded favorably to this offer of hope from one of their own kind; the next weekend, attendance in Roy's Bible study doubled. Roy was pleased by the boys' response, but it frustrated him to see the teenagers return to their old environment after their release. There was no follow-up program, no way to prevent them from slipping back into old habits and self-destructive life-styles.

Then, one day after reading David Wilkerson's book *The Cross and the Switchblade,* Roy saw his answer. He could refer boys from camp and Juvenile Hall to a Teen Challenge Center for help. He located the Center in Los Angeles, got acquainted with the people who ran it, and became involved with the Teen Challenge work. Director Don Hall helped Roy institute a program whereby certain juveniles were released directly to Teen Challenge headquarters for intensive rehabilitation therapy.

That summer Don Hall introduced Roy to David Wilkerson. The two men felt an immediate rapport; they spent time together talking and discussing their mutual goals for teens and the Teen Challenge ministry. In the fall Roy began to set up crusades for David in the Southern California area—Los Angeles, San Diego, San Bernardino, Fresno, Bakersfield. He organized the programs, reserved the auditoriums, handled all the behind-the-scenes details, then traveled with David to the various meetings. The two began to talk about the possibility of Roy becoming Wilkerson's full-time crusade director, to set up meetings all over the country. It was something they would both consider seriously and pray about in the days ahead.

In the spring of 1964 Wanda had wonderful news for Roy. She was going to have a baby in October.

Roy was delighted. "A baby? That's great!" He hugged her excitedly. "What shall we have—a girl? How about a daughter first!"

Wanda laughed. "I think that's already been decided. But yes, a daughter would be wonderful."

Roy's expression grew thoughtful. "Maybe we should think now about putting down roots, maybe buying a house."

Wanda smiled wistfully. Yes, she wanted roots, longed for them. "It would be super. But there's no way we can afford a house now with a baby coming."

Her words were very nearly prophetic.

Wanda had a difficult pregnancy and was forced to give up her job. To make ends meet, Roy dropped out of Biola College and began working for Prudential Life Insurance. He did extraordinarily well. In a short time their financial situation had improved enough that he and Wanda decided to buy a home after all.

With a five-hundred dollar down payment, they purchased a large old house in Whittier. It was a pleasant home with four bedrooms. The best part was that it was theirs. It appeared they would be able to live a fairly settled life for a change.

As the months of Wanda's pregnancy crept by, she felt increasingly miserable. Late summer heat only aggravated her

discomfort. One afternoon, seeking to cool off, she soaked
leisurely in the bathtub. But when she tried to climb out, her
swollen body was too awkward and heavy to manage even this
simple task. Suddenly she felt incredibly angry over being
pregnant. If only she could forget the whole thing! She began to
sob uncontrollably, hating herself, hating the whole wretched
world. A puzzled, alarmed Roy came dashing to her rescue. He
dragged her clumsily out of the tub and attempted, with little
success, to calm her down. Then he prayed with her—prayed
she would get her attitude straightened out. The last thing on
earth Wanda wanted at that moment was to pray. She wanted
sympathy—and a towel. Not a sermon!

On a Friday in September, nearly a month before the baby
was due, Wanda went in for her regular doctor's appointment
and learned she was suffering from toxemia, a blood poisoning
which threatened the life of her unborn child. "I want you to
check into the hospital on Monday," the doctor told her.

But on Sunday her water broke. Roy was working, so Wanda,
fighting anxiety, telephoned her parents. They came immediately
and took her to the hospital. Roy arrived shortly and spent the
evening with her. They played Rook to pass the time, but it was
clear nothing was happening. Wanda wasn't in labor.

Finally the doctor came in and said, "It's not going to happen
tonight. Go home, Mr. Comstock, and come back in the
morning. She's doing fine." So Roy went home.

When he returned at 7:30 the next morning, Wanda was
already in hard labor. The exhausting birth pangs lasted over
four hours. Wanda screamed as her body was assaulted by
waves of pain. It was a long, difficult delivery, but at 11:30 A.M.,
September 22, 1964, Denise Eileen Comstock made her
entrance, kicking and bawling lustily.

She was a pretty baby. Roy was pleased; he had seen so
many ugly babies, but Denise was pretty. She was a good baby
too; she slept at night and wasn't fussy. Both Roy and Wanda
felt blessed to have her.

But Wanda did not regain her strength easily or quickly. When
she came home from the hospital, she stayed in bed much of the
time. Her mother moved in for several weeks to care for both
Wanda and Denise. But Wanda's health would get worse before
it got better.

CHAPTER TWENTY

As the Thanksgiving holidays approached, Roy found himself increasingly involved in David Wilkerson's Southern California crusades. He knew he was going to have to make a decision soon about whether or not to become Wilkerson's national crusade director. One night he told Wanda, "Dave wants me to go back to New York with him this coming weekend to see the operation there, meet the people, and get some direction as to what God wants us to do. Will you and the baby be all right without me?"

Wanda nodded. "I know you have to go. It's the only way you'll have peace about where God wants us."

The night before Roy was to leave for New York, Wanda awoke with severe abdominal pains. Roy called her parents, who came and picked up Denise while Roy rushed Wanda to the hospital. There the doctor assured Roy that her condition was not serious and that he could go ahead with his trip.

Roy wasn't convinced. He took Wanda's hand and asked, "Honey, do you want me to stay?"

"No," she murmured. "You go ahead. I'll be OK."

Reassured, Roy flew to New York with Wilkerson early the next morning. But when he telephoned Wanda that evening from David's home, he received a cryptic reply from the hospital switchboard operator. "I'm sorry. Mrs. Comstock is unable to speak to anyone."

"Then let me talk to her doctor," Roy insisted.

After a long delay, the doctor came on the line and said, "Well, Mr. Comstock, it was more serious than we thought."

"What do you mean?" Roy demanded. "How serious?"

Another interminable pause. Then the husky reply: "We could have lost her."

"What do you mean?" cried Roy, a jagged fear lurching inside him.

The doctor was noncommital. "I anticipate her doing better."

Roy struggled to collect his thoughts. "What happened to her, doctor? She seemed all right last night."

"It's an unusual situation," the doctor replied. "There's probably a million to one chance of it occurring. A hemorrhagic cyst, probably related to the childbirth, has ruptured. There's internal bleeding. We're hoping surgery won't be necessary. I suggest you call back in a few hours. I'll be able to tell you more then."

Roy hung up the telephone and looked at David in stunned disbelief. "Dave, my wife is really very sick."

David gripped Roy's shoulder. "Well, let's pray for Wanda right now," he suggested. Together they knelt and asked God to touch Wanda's body and heal her.

When Roy telephoned the hospital a few hours later, the doctor said, "We've passed the danger period. The bleeding stopped—rather suddenly, in fact. She's going to be OK."

On Monday Roy returned from New York and picked Wanda up at the hospital. "We'll let her go home now if you'll keep her in bed for several days," the doctor told him.

Driving home, Roy asked, "Are you feeling OK, Honey?"

"I think so," she replied weakly. "I don't remember much about the last couple days. It was like the lights were suddenly turned out. Everything went blank. When I woke up yesterday, Mom and Dad were sitting there looking terribly worried. They said I had been critical, but then the bleeding stopped just like that. I have this feeling, Roy—I think it was a miracle."

Roy squeezed her knee affectionately. "I know it was."

Wanda studied his expression. "Your trip—did it help you to decide?"

"Not really," admitted Roy. "I'm excited about Dave's work, but I just don't know if God wants me to be part of it." He smiled. "It was kind of funny. They jokingly called me a 'Bapticost' at Wilkerson's headquarters. But Dave and I both know I'm just a plain old Baptist."

"So what are you going to do?"

"Wait, I guess. And pray. Dave's praying too. If we feel God is saying yes, if we feel we can really work together, we'll write each other." He looked at her closely. "Wanda, I'm really sorry I wasn't with you through all this. You know that, don't you?"

Wanda stared passively at her hands. "Yes, I know." Her voice fell to a whisper. "I know you were doing what you had to do."

Roy ground his jaw slightly. "Wanda, I think your folks were angry with me for going to New York when you were ill. I hope you're not angry too."

Wanda shook her head wearily. "I said I understand, Roy. And I think Mom and Dad were more worried than angry."

"I hope so, Hon." They rode in silence for a while; then Roy said, "I think I'll go see my mother this week. Show her the new pictures of the baby."

"She'd like that," Wanda agreed. "She's probably pretty lonely. After being in the hospital myself, I know how nice it is to have visitors."

Bertha Comstock had been in and out of the hospital constantly over the past three years. Now she was confined to a TB ward in a Long Beach hospital, her condition complicated by diabetes and cervical cancer. Roy visited her often, sometimes reading from the Scriptures or playing records of the New Testament on his portable phonograph.

Over the past several years Bertha had developed an almost obsessive interest in religion. She read the Bible, listened to religious radio and TV programs, and filled her letters with so many Scripture verses her children scarcely read them anymore. But she believed in a religion of good works. She refused to listen when Roy brought up the subject of salvation through faith in Christ.

When Roy went to visit his mother that week, their conversation took an unexpected turn. Bertha, her cheeks hollow, her face drawn, lay quietly gazing at photographs of her new granddaughter. "Oh, she's so sweet . . . so sweet," she whispered over and over.

Talking about Denise's birth opened a special door of communication between Roy and his mother. They talked about the miracle of life and birth; then Roy moved on to the subject of the *new* birth. "You know, Mom," he said, "just as we're born physically, so we need to be born spiritually to be a member of God's family. It's not something we can do just by living right. Christ has to give us life—his life."

For the first time Bertha wasn't on the defensive. "I've tried so hard," she murmured sadly. "I've tried to make up for everything. I never knew if it was enough."

Roy took his mother's small, frail hand in his. "Mom, did you ever stop to think that if we could live good enough lives to please God, then Christ wouldn't have had to die? He came to do something for us we couldn't do for ourselves. It's only through his death and resurrection that we can be born again and become children of God. Listen to this, Mom," he added, opening his Bible and reading from John 3 about the encounter between Jesus and Nicodemus.

When Roy had finished reading, Bertha smiled wanly, "I think I understand, Son. I can't save myself."

"That's right, Mom." In the next few minutes Roy knelt beside his mother's bed and prayed; then Bertha prayed, quietly making Christ her own.

When Roy returned home that evening, he felt as if something crucial in the scheme of things had come full circle. A quarter century ago Bertha had given him life; now he had had the awesome privilege of helping her find eternal life in Christ.

CHAPTER TWENTY-ONE

Just before Christmas Roy received a call from Bob Hart, his good friend from Bethel College days. "Roy, we've got our headquarters for the American Evangelism Association set up here in St. Paul," he said, "and we're ready now to call our first staff evangelist. I'd like you to pray about who that man should be."

"Sure, Bob, I'll be praying," replied Roy. This wasn't his first occasion to hear about the American Evangelism Association. In September, shortly before Denise's birth, Roy had flown to Omaha to help Bob lay the foundation for the new ministry.

"You know, Roy," continued Bob, "this position doesn't require seminary training. With your zeal for evangelistic work, maybe you should consider joining us."

Roy hesitated only a moment, then replied, "Don't think I haven't thought about it, Bob. As you know, I've been considering going with Dave Wilkerson. I'll tell you what; I'll talk it over with Wanda. We'll pray about it, and I'll get back with you."

Surprisingly, Wanda was as excited as Roy over the idea of joining the new ministry in Minnesota. They had been through this dilemma often enough before—Roy's tug of war between business and evangelism. They both preferred evangelism.

"It will mean selling the house and all our new furniture," warned Roy. "Not to mention living on a lower income."

"That's OK," Wanda assured him. "I'm happy when I see you excited about the Lord's work."

When Roy telephoned Bob, Bob's first question was, "Are you coming to Minnesota?"

"Yep, we're coming!" said Roy. "Give us a week. We'll be on our way. We've written to Dave Wilkerson, letting him know our decision."

Wanda was stunned by the idea of leaving in one short week. There was so much to do—pack, break the news to relatives, sell the house and furniture. Besides, Denise was only three months old and Wanda had just begun to regain her strength.

But Roy, having confirmed the decision to go, was already there in spirit, relishing the vision of ministry. Mundane details of packing and disposing of property were minor obstacles to be scaled swiftly, boldly. He accepted the first offer on the house. Then when someone handed him a five hundred dollar check for all the furniture, Roy answered, "Sold!"

Wanda watched in silent horror as the transaction was completed. Surely their furniture was worth much, much more. The stove alone was worth five-hundred dollars! Wanda turned in anger and revulsion and ran into the bedroom, quickly shutting the door behind her.

Roy came in a few minutes later, waving the check and grinning. "Well, we just got rid of our debts, Hon. We're free to go!"

Wanda forced herself to remain calm. "Couldn't we have gotten more for the furniture?" she questioned. "The washer, the dryer, the refrigerator, the stove—they were all brand-new. Everything together should be worth a couple thousand dollars."

"I just wanted enough to cover what we still owed on them," Roy explained. "I didn't want to be tied down with a lot of stuff when we're leaving next week."

Wanda looked away, blinking back hot tears of frustration. "I—I better go check on Denise," she said coolly, escaping to the other room.

Roy's only regret in leaving California was that he would be going away just when he and his mother had found a new closeness in their mutual faith. Just before leaving for Minnesota, he went to see his mother again. Talking with Bertha, he was pleased to learn she had already led a couple of the nurses to the Lord. He was happy to see the joy in her face, the sparkle in her eyes as she talked about what God was doing in her life.

After Roy told her of his plans to move away, they were both momentarily silent, realizing the likelihood that they would not see each other again. "Mom, no matter what happens to us here on earth," said Roy, "isn't it wonderful to know that someday we'll be together in heaven with Christ?"

She nodded, then reached out for his hand. "You know, Son, I've been praying for Milt," she said slowly. "I'm not going to get to see him."

"Sure you will, Mom."

"No, I won't." She paused, her breathing labored, then looked at him with an intensity in her eyes he had never seen before. "You've got to tell Milt about Jesus, Roy."

He nodded, but he wasn't sure how or when he would keep the promise. They talked a few minutes more, said their goodbyes, then Roy got up to leave.

Bertha's last words to him as he walked out the door were, "You've got to tell Milt, Roy."

"I will, Mom," he told her.

It was the last time Roy would see his mother alive. In August 1965, while Roy was still in Minnesota, he would receive word from his father of her death. He and Wanda would fly back for the funeral; it would not be a time of sorrow or tears, for Roy would be able to look at his mother and say with full assurance, "I'll see you later, Mom."

On January 11, 1965, Roy, Wanda, and Denise arrived in St. Paul, pulling a U-Haul trailer behind their 1962 Ford. They stayed at first with Bob and LuAnn Hart, then moved into a tiny second-story apartment on noisy, busy Snelling Avenue. Their furniture consisted of a hide-a-bed, a chair, and a crib.

Wanda, who had never traveled beyond the California border, found Minnesota to be both beautiful and cold. But she was disappointed that there was no snow on the ground. One night shortly after their arrival, Roy overheard her praying for snow. At twenty-one, she had never seen a snowfall. A few days later it began to snow—and snowed straight through until April! People who had heard Roy mention Wanda's prayer began to telephone the house and ask her to please stop praying for snow. They'd had enough!

Roy stepped immediately into his new role as staff evangelist. The American Evangelism Association was vitally involved in what Bob and Roy called "grass roots" evangelism. They went into churches and trained laymen in soul-winning through door-to-door, person-to-person contacts. They also held week-long crusades during which persons completing the training classes served as counselors, praying with those who came forward to accept Christ. On each Friday night, usually tagged "teen night," the young people gathered to play volleyball or basketball, and to enjoy a time of fellowship. On Saturdays, if the weather was warm enough, Roy, Bob, and members of the training classes went to parks and beaches, doing outdoor evangelism.

Wanda always bundled up Denise and went along with Roy to the meetings. She began to think it was the only way to see her husband, since he was gone nearly every evening. In spite of her bouts with loneliness, she tried to compensate, tried to keep her eyes on what God was accomplishing in their ministry. Hundreds of people were learning about being soul winners, and hundreds more were professing salvation in Christ. It was an exciting time for both Wanda and Roy.

Exciting—but also extremely difficult. There was so little money. No steady support. Scarcely enough to eat. Perhaps because their ministry was mainly behind the scenes, it wasn't glamorous enough to prompt people to underwrite it. Or maybe support was lacking because they ministered primarily in small, financially struggling churches. Whatever the reason, Roy and Wanda found themselves in debt again, lacking money even for the necessities of life.

One evening they sat facing each other over a meager dinner of macaroni and coffee. Wanda answered Roy's questioning gaze with a discouraged sigh. "There's no money for food," she said. "I spent our last dollar on milk for Denise. I don't know what we'll do tomorrow."

Roy raked his fingers through his hair in a stymied, preoccupied gesture. He hated feeling helpless. There had to be some answer to their dilemma. "I believe we're where God wants us," he told Wanda fervently, "and I don't feel we should have to struggle like this for money. I believe God will supply our needs."

"I believe that too," said Wanda, "but we don't have any more food. Denise isn't eating right. None of us are."

Roy stirred his coffee perfunctorily. "It's just not as easy as I thought to get started as an evangelist. I suppose it's like this for missionaries, too." He put his spoon down on the saucer and lifted his cup. "You want to concentrate on preaching the Word, but then you have to stop and wonder how you're going to eat, who's going to pay the bills."

Wanda gazed wistfully at Roy as he sipped his coffee. "Wouldn't it be neat if all the Christians who have a good income would really get involved in supporting new ministries like ours? Think what we could do!"

"It doesn't work that way," said Roy. "People just aren't aware! Or they don't have the burden. I don't know. Whatever it is, I—I'm going to have to go back to sales work if things don't change."

In April Roy did take a secular job. He had no choice; his 1962 Ford had been repossessed, so he had no transportation. By becoming a salesman for a Dodge dealership, he had unlimited access to a demonstrator car—a little red Simca. He also received a much-needed weekly salary of one hundred dollars.

Roy continued to serve as staff evangelist for the American Evangelism Association, preaching nightly after selling automobiles during the day. It was a grueling schedule—no less so for Wanda who, finding a sitter for Denise, began working for the Metropolitan Planning Commission of Minneapolis-St. Paul, typing reports and doing routine office work.

But their problems were far from solved. One cold, wet afternoon toward the end of April, Wanda was driving to the Dodge dealership to pick up Roy. The roads were icy, the traffic congested. When the automobiles in front of her stopped suddenly, Wanda put on the brakes, too. But the truck behind her didn't stop. Instead, it slammed into the rear end of the Simca with a sudden, strong jolt.

Both Wanda and the truck driver climbed out of their vehicles and stared dumbfounded at the crumpled metal.

"I'm awfully sorry, Ma'am," the driver said unsteadily. "My feet were wet, so when I stepped on the brake, my foot slipped off and hit the gas pedal instead. Are you OK?"

"Yes, I think so," Wanda replied vaguely. After exchanging insurance information with the man, she climbed back into the car. "I have to go. My husband's waiting for me to pick him up."

"Lady, you're trembling. You sure you're up to driving?"

"Yes, I told you—I'm fine."

But she wasn't fine. She had received a severe whiplash, the pain radiating down her entire spine. For several months she had to wear a special collar and undergo therapy treatments regularly. She remained in great discomfort. Still, it was something she was able to live with—until Thanksgiving.

For Thanksgiving, Roy had invited several friends from Bethel Seminary over for dinner. Wanda prepared a big turkey with all the trimmings, but the celebration was cut short. Just after dinner, Wanda sat down hard on the couch, accidentally bruising her tailbone. She was suddenly in such excruciating pain she couldn't move.

"It's my old back injury," she gasped. "Only this time it's really bad."

Someone mentioned going to the hospital, but Wanda said no. She decided to endure the pain until the next day when her doctor would be in the office. And she wanted to stay close to Denise, who had been fussy and running a fever for two days.

The next morning Wanda was still doubled over, unable to move. And Denise had developed a rash and was running a temperature of 104°. Roy drove Wanda to the doctor, carrying her out to the car and back.

"I'm admitting her to Midway Hospital for traction this afternoon," the doctor told Roy. "If that doesn't work we may have to try surgery. I'm not sure her back will ever be normal again."

Roy and Wanda returned to their apartment to pick up a few things for her hospital stay. While there, Denise went into convulsions. Frightened, Roy telephoned Wanda's doctor. "Get her over to Children's Hospital right away," he told Roy.

A half hour later Roy admitted Denise at Children's Hospital in St. Paul and then delivered Wanda to Midway. He spent the next ten days commuting between the two hospitals, visiting Wanda, who had her legs up in traction, and Denise, who lay burning with fever, scarcely able to breathe.

Denise, hardly more than a year old, was the more seriously ill of the two. Suffering from a severe case of roseola, she was dehydrated and her fever remained dangerously high in spite of efforts to bring it down. If her fever didn't break soon, she could die. Roy spent as much time with his child as possible, sitting beside her crib, watching her, praying.

When Roy went to see Wanda and she asked where he had been, he carefully changed the subject. He didn't want her to know how much time he was spending at Children's Hospital.

"I feel so bad that I can't go see Denise," Wanda would sigh. "She's so little and so alone."

Roy would nod, silent; he couldn't share just how frightened he was for their tiny daughter's life.

Roy, refusing to give in to his fears for his family, continued to hold evening crusades. One night he was scheduled to speak at a youth rally. Before the service he called together the young people from the evangelism training class and asked them to pray with him for Denise. The teenagers sat down and prayed one by one. When Roy went over to the hospital after the meeting, the doctor on duty greeted him with a relieved grin. "Well, your daughter's fever has finally broken," he said. "It looks like she's going to be OK."

Once again God had honored the prayers of his children for healing.

Both Wanda and Denise were home in time for Christmas. But new turmoils plagued the Comstock household. Wanda was terribly homesick. This was her first Christmas away from her family. She spent the day crying. The trials of the past year—the financial struggles, the unrelenting physical pain, the loneliness, the worries over Denise—all struck her now with sudden force. To make matters worse, she dreaded facing another Minnesota winter.

"I'm so cold all the time," she told Roy. "And I'm afraid to drive on the ice with my bad back. If I get hit again there could be permanent damage. I might not be able to walk again." Her voice broke. "I miss living in California where it's warm. And I really miss my folks."

Roy understood. He too was homesick. As much as he loved preaching, the past year had shown him he couldn't support himself in evangelism; he had to keep going back to the business world. In the past couple of months he had left the Dodge dealership to begin selling motivational programs, tapes, and records for Success Motivation Institute. In a short time he was doing extremely well, making good money. Now he was trying to analyze the circumstances, to understand just what God was trying to tell him.

The day after Christmas, Roy sat down with Wanda to discuss their future. He put his arm around her and pulled her close, the way he always did when he had something important to say. "I've been praying about this for weeks," he told her, "and I finally have peace about what God wants me to do. I think the Lord gave us the experience of this past year to show us how difficult it is to get started in evangelism." He shook his head soberly. "We've seen firsthand that people going into the ministry have certain hardships and difficulties and problems that no one knows who hasn't been through them."

"We've certainly learned that lesson," Wanda agreed, resting her head against him.

"Well, Hon, God has given me a burden to help support young evangelists—those struggling just as we've struggled this past year. I'm going back into sales. I believe God has given me the ability to do well in business. I'm going to trust him to give me enough money to underwrite others who are called into evangelism."

Wanda nodded reflectively. "It does sound right for us. You've felt the pull between business and evangelism for so long; now we've experienced both sides." She looked at him intently. "Does this mean we're going home to California?"

"Yes, Hon," he said, embracing her, laughing. "It means just that. We're going home!"

CHAPTER TWENTY-TWO

If Roy and Wanda thought their year in Minnesota was difficult, they hadn't seen anything yet. Preparing to return to California, both were buoyed by grand hopes for the future. Surely they had been through the valley of the shadow; now they were climbing to higher ground. Or were they?

On New Year's Eve, Wanda and Denise flew home to California while Roy drove to Waco, Texas, for a one-week training session in the Success Motivation Institute. Together with Darrell Johnson, his buddy from Bethel who was also on the American Evangelism staff, Roy borrowed ten thousand dollars from Darrell's father-in-law to purchase a franchise in the Success Motivation Institute. After completing the course, Roy returned to California, moved his little family into a luxury apartment in Whittier, and established his franchise under the name CITA ("Christ Is The Answer") Enterprises, selling SMI programs for training personnel in sales techniques, positive thinking attitudes, motivation, and perseverance.

The Institute's mode of operation dictated that each franchise holder recruit, hire, and train men under him to sell the programs to still other salesmen who would eventually offer the programs to industry. Roy, unimpressed by this "pyramid" approach, preferred to peddle the programs directly to local corporations. He spent his days—and yes, evenings, too—calling on businesses and prospective buyers, while Wanda handled all the bookwork at home.

But even with their borrowed ten thousand dollars, they didn't have the working capital to keep things going. In two months they were two months behind in rent, and were forced to move into a cramped house in an older section of town. Their debts were mounting rapidly; not a penny was coming in. Tension in the Comstock household mushroomed almost as swiftly as their mountain of debts.

"I knew you never should have borrowed all that money from Darrell's father-in-law," Wanda lamented one evening after Roy's expression told her it had been another "no sale" day. "How will we ever pay him back?"

Roy slammed his briefcase against the couch. "Well, I'm out day and night trying to sell these blasted programs. Can I help it nobody will buy? SMI expects me to know everything about the business after one lousy week of training. They keep saying, 'How many people have you hired, how many kits have you sold?' Honey, you know I tried hiring a couple of guys a while back, but they just didn't work out."

"But we can't do it, Roy, just the two of us," protested Wanda. "It's been almost six months and you've sold only a couple of programs. How much longer can we hold on?"

Roy loosened his tie and pulled it off in a quick, unyielding gesture. "I'm not giving up, Wanda," he said shortly. "I know God wants me to be a success in business so I can help support evangelism."

Wanda turned away abruptly. "You can't even support your own family," she muttered under her breath.

"I've got to do this for the Lord," Roy shot back fiercely. "I know we'll make it if we just hang on a few more months."

Wanda looked back at him, her expression grave. "Have you stopped to think you might be doing the wrong thing? Maybe it's time for you to get a regular nine-to-five job. You said R. B. Furniture offered you a position."

Roy stared at her with an intensity that made her flinch. "I told you I'm not going to work for anyone else. I'm going to make a go of this thing!"

Without a reply, Wanda strode to the kitchen and opened the cupboard. "One of us has to bring in some money," she said, taking out a box of cereal. "So I'm going back to work."

Roy followed her into the kitchen and took the cereal. "What do you mean? Work—where?"

"Westland Associates—the wholesale house near here. They need a receptionist-biller." She removed a bottle of milk from the refrigerator and set it on the table. "Roy, I haven't given them my decision yet, but I think I should take the job."

Roy gazed soberly at the box in his hand. "This is our dinner? Cold cereal again?"

Wanda gave a futile nod toward the open cupboard. "There's nothing else, Roy. Nothing. See for yourself."

He sat down with sudden heaviness. "OK, Wanda. Take the job . . . at least until I get on my feet."

In spite of Wanda's modest income, the next six months were far more desperate for the Comstocks than the previous six. By the end of 1966, they had lost seventeen thousand dollars, seven of which they didn't have to start with.

The pressures on both Wanda and Roy were incredible—and too often left unspoken. It was as if they occupied opposing camps over which loomed an uneasy truce. Roy was all too aware that he wasn't bringing in any money, his debts were skyrocketing, and he had failed his family and friends who had invested so much in him. Worst of all, he had made a farce of his own treasured vision of serving God by supporting evangelistic efforts.

Wanda managed to disregard her unhappiness while at work each day; she was much too busy to dwell on her problems. But each time she picked up Denise at preschool and began the drive home, an oppressive gloom inevitably shrouded her spirits. She couldn't tell Roy how terrible she felt, how upsetting it was for a girl who had never owed a penny before her marriage to be so hopelessly in debt to so many. To speak of her distress would only increase Roy's misery. Like Roy, she refused to admit they were on a collision course with each other, with their creditors, and with God.

Then it happened. The inescapable rupture. Too many frayed seams . . . frayed nerves . . . tattered dreams. Wanda walked out.

She left early one evening in January 1967. That morning, before leaving for work, she had received a phone call from the electric company; their electricity would be turned off unless they paid their bill immediately. Two days earlier she had received notice that their water would be shut off in five days. They were two months behind in their rent, too. Why couldn't Roy see that their world was collapsing around them?

When Wanda returned home from work, she faced the worst shock yet. The furniture was gone; it had been repossessed. And there was an ominous notice in the mail from the finance company: someone was coming to pick up their car; it too was being reclaimed.

Wanda crumpled the notice with trembling fingers. Tears welled in her eyes and spilled out uncontrollably. "It isn't fair," she said aloud. "This is Roy's problem! He's not providing for us." She looked around frantically. "Oh, God, I don't want to be here when they turn off the lights and the gas. I don't want to see them take the car!"

She stooped down and gathered Denise into her arms. The toddler patted her cheek uncomprehendingly. "We've got to go away, Denise," said Wanda. "I've got to get out of here."

Denise smiled. "Go where, Mama?"

"I don't know, Honey." Wanda stood up and scooted the child toward the bedroom. "Go get some of your toys, Sweetie. We're going to—to Grandma's." She reached for the telephone. Did she dare go through with it—leave Roy, go home to her folks? Fresh tears sprang to her eyes. "Oh, God," she whispered urgently, "I don't know if I even love him anymore!"

With a decisiveness bordering on desperation, Wanda telephoned her parents. "Mother, I—I want to come home," she said falteringly. "I can't take any more."

Her parents were more than sympathetic. They assured her they would come immediately. Wanda hung up the receiver, feeling a mixture of humiliation and relief. She packed a few clothes, scribbled a note to Roy, and propped it on his pillow.

Riding home with her folks, Wanda cried again—cried for the lost hopes and broken dreams. She and Roy had counted on so much; now so little seemed to remain.

Her parents were visibly upset. "I knew this was bound to happen," said her mother. "Roy's not a responsible person, Wanda. He's just no good for you. It's time you realized that."

"That dirty dog's not doing right by you, that's for sure," her father added severely. "He's a failure, unstable, just like his father."

"He's not like his father," Wanda started to protest, then fell silent, realizing suddenly how alike Roy and his father really were.

"Well, he's certainly a weak man, Wanda," her mother pressed on. "You're better off without him."

Wanda swallowed a sob. "No, no, you're both wrong. He's not weak. He's tried and tried to make a go of things. Daddy, he's a good man. I know he is. He can't help what's happened."

"If he can't, then who can?" her father returned sharply.

After dinner that evening, Wanda sat down beside her folks. She rubbed her hands distractedly. They felt cold, cold to the bone; she couldn't make them warm. "I don't know what I'm going to do," she said quietly, "but I realized tonight that I still love Roy."

Her father nodded, his brow creased in consternation. "Obviously," he sighed. "We knew that by the way you defended him in the car."

"But I'm so tired, Daddy, so terribly, terribly tired."

"Go to bed now, Dear," said her mother soothingly, as she sat rocking Denise. "Think about things tomorrow."

Wanda slept on a hide-a-bed in her old room, which had been made over into a den now, but was still somehow comfortingly, nostalgically familiar. She felt as though she could sleep for a thousand years.

When Roy returned home late that night, he found the house strangely still. And empty. He went from room to room turning on lights, calling Wanda's name. In the bedroom he found her note—a fragile, inconspicuous missive: *Roy, I've taken Denise and gone to my folks. I'm sorry, but I can't live like this anymore. Wanda.*

Roy sat down on the bed, stunned. Something lurched inside him. He suffered a sudden pain of loss, almost a physical blow. Comprehension struck with devastating impact: *I've really blown it this time. Wanda . . . Denise . . . Everything worthwhile is gone.*

He stood up and paced the room, sat down a moment, then stood up again. What was he going to do? Go after Wanda? It was too late. He couldn't risk creating a scene at her parents' home. No, let her be. For tonight anyway.

He sat back down on the bed and put his head in his hands. "God, what are you doing to me?" he said aloud. "What is it you want from me? I have tried—oh, God, I've tried!"

He stood up again, restless, angry, baffled. He went about the house turning off lights, then returned to the darkness of the bedroom. He stood in silence, aware of the muted groanings of the house and staccato street sounds outside—the whir of traffic, a car backfiring, the solitary blast of a horn. It had been years since Roy had felt so alone, so cut off, so desolate.

He knelt beside his bed and stared up into the blackness. "God, what did I do wrong? I prayed about going into evangelism. I prayed about going into business. I thought I was doing what you wanted. I was so sure! But I've failed miserably at both." He sighed heavily. "Lord, I don't know what to do. I don't know where to turn." He shook his head slowly, ponderously, trying to sort his thoughts. "Father, I wanted so much to be successful so that I could help people in the ministry. Was that wrong? Did I want it too much?" He put his head in his hands, choking back a sudden surge of emotion. "Oh, God, I can't let go of it; I can't let that dream pass out of my hands. I don't want to fail!"

He stopped praying for a moment and considered what he was saying. *What I want . . . what I don't want . . . what I've tried to do.* "That's it, isn't it, Father," he said suddenly. "My own stubborn will. I want desperately to succeed, but I'm not willing to fail." He almost laughed aloud, the answer was so obvious. "Lord, this isn't easy, but . . . OK, I'll do whatever you want me to do. I'm willing . . . yes, I'm willing even to fail—to accept my failure—if that's what pleases you."

Just saying the words brought a sense of release. Surrender— that was the key. Being willing to please God however *he* chose, not how Roy Comstock dictated. Immense relief came in knowing Christ was back in control, holding the reins. Roy felt at peace for the first time in months.

With the newfound peace came the answer he had sought—as clearly as if God were whispering the words: *Roy, you don't have to fail. You are where I want you to be. The problem is that you're doing it instead of me. You need to step aside and let me work through you.*

So that was it. There was nothing wrong with success if you let Christ accomplish it through you. In the hours that followed, Roy sealed his commitment with God, renewing his faith, praising his Savior.

As morning dawned, Roy realized he had prayed all night. He was emotionally drained and physically exhausted; every muscle in his body ached. But he would remember this time of prayer as a major turning point in his life.

CHAPTER TWENTY-THREE

The telephone jangled.

"Westland Associates," replied Wanda, in her business voice.

"Wanda, this is Roy."

Silence.

"Wanda, did you hear me? I've got to talk to you."

"I—I can't talk now."

"When are you coming home?"

Pause. "I don't know, Roy. I really don't want to go back . . ."

"Don't want to—?"

"But I can't stay with my parents either."

Roy's voice came back angry, wounded. "Well, if you don't want to come home, you can just stay with your folks!"

"No, I don't want to, Roy. I don't know what to do." She began to cry.

Roy's tone softened. "Listen, Wanda, I'm not saying what I want to say. I want you to know—I prayed last night, and I'm willing to do whatever it takes to make things right between us."

Wanda's voice was tentative. "Will you get a regular nine-to-five job?"

He sighed heavily. "Yeah, Hon, even that."

"Then I'll try again," said Wanda.

After work that evening Roy picked Wanda up and together they went after Denise. Roy kept his promise. He became a sales representative for Coast Envelope Company; it was a salaried job with regular hours.

Wanda was pleased. In the next three months they were able to pay off some of their bills and even save a few dollars. They wrote letters to their major creditors, including Darrell's father-in-law, explaining that they would be paying a certain amount toward their debt each month. The future looked promising, almost secure.

But by early April Wanda knew something was wrong. Roy was restless and irritable. Worst of all, he was talking about going back into sales. She refused to listen.

One night their precarious illusion of peace and tranquillity toppled. Wanda was clearing the table after supper when Roy casually mentioned his intention to start selling Kirby vacuum cleaners. "I thought I'd start out selling just in the evenings," he said. Wanda turned away, but he could tell by the way her back stiffened that she was against the idea.

"Wanda, you know this nine-to-five routine is driving me absolutely nuts," he told her. Without a word she wiped her hands on a dish towel and went into the living room. He followed her. "Wanda, do you hear me? I said I can't take this—"

"I hear you," she said, "but I can't take your going back into commission selling. Don't you understand? I need to see that paycheck. I need to know the money will be coming in."

"And I've got to escape this deadening sameness," he countered. "I feel like a caged lion."

"You've been *acting* like a caged lion for weeks," she retorted.

Roy waved his hand in a gesture of rebuke. His expression was strained, intense. "Look, Wanda, I'm going back into sales. That's it. You're either going to have to accept me the way I am and we make it from there, or we go our separate ways. Those are the conditions."

Wanda stared at Roy in disbelief. She felt as if she had been knocked to the floor; and now somehow she couldn't quite catch her breath. "OK," she murmured numbly, "if that's how it is, I'll go along with whatever you say."

He managed a tilted smile. "It'll be OK, Wanda. You wait and see. We're going to make it this time."

The next day Roy went to work for Kirby, selling in the evenings while completing his last few weeks for Coast Envelope. He did well at sales—just as he said he would. Near the end of April, when he and Wanda received a five-hundred dollar refund from income taxes, they went out and purchased a lovely new home in Rowland Heights.

But before long, Wanda hated it. The house was away from everything, "out in the boondocks," as she called it. She felt alone, alienated from the whole world. So after a few months, she and Roy decided to move on.

In the months that followed, they made a series of moves—to a tiny apartment in Hollywood (the landlord didn't like children); then to a place in Long Beach (they were too close for comfort to their families); and finally to an apartment in Beverly Hills.

Roy's career with Kirby began to soar. He became an associate divisional supervisor, was put on salary plus overrides and bonuses, and began traveling all over the Southern California region, hiring and training salesmen and holding motivational meetings (applying some of his knowledge and experience from SMI days). He was making better money than he had ever made before. At last Wanda was able to quit her job and stay home with Denise.

Then early in 1968 their lives unexpectedly changed direction again. Roy and Wanda were celebrating their fifth anniversary over a romantic dinner for two in a special restaurant. Their friends Dean and Mary Jean Brown happened to be eating there, too. As the two couples chatted briefly, Dean told Roy about his part-time work for Audio Bible Studies. "Earle Williams is looking for a sales manager," added Dean. "He needs a Christian who knows something about sales, to head things up. It's really a unique opportunity."

Roy was immediately interested. "It sounds like a great way to combine a ministry with sales."

"That's the beauty of it," said Dean.

Wanda gave Roy a hopeful glance. "Honey, it sounds like what we've been praying for."

The following week, Roy telephoned Earle Williams, founder-director of the Bible teaching ministry, introduced himself, and set up an appointment. The two met; Earle showed Roy the operation; they prayed together about Roy's possible future with the organization. It didn't take long for Roy to make his decision. This time he and Wanda were in total agreement: God wanted him with Audio Bible Studies.

Roy's new position as national sales manager gave him his first opportunity to create a whole concept—to put together an entire sales presentation and distributorship program. He began traveling all over the United States, hiring and training sales people, speaking on dozens of local radio stations, and selling distributorships in Audio Bible Studies.

The following year, the organization thrived—and so did Roy and Wanda. Their lives were fruitful and happy; their marriage was good. It was a fun time. Wanda basked in their new financial security; Roy relished the experience of developing a sales organization on his own. Indeed, for Roy, it was a spiraling year, a graduate school in experience.

It wasn't long before Roy and Wanda were able to afford another home. With one month's earnings they put a down payment on a beautiful new house in Brea. Then they went out and bought all new furniture. Their days of poverty and strife were very nearly forgotten.

The only blight on their joy was that Roy had to spend more and more time traveling away from home. Often he was gone three weeks at a time to set up a distributorship in some far-flung section of the country. Neither Roy nor Wanda could tolerate the lengthy absences. After the third week of such absences, Wanda's nerves were perilously on edge, and Roy found that his desire to work had dissipated; he could concentrate only on getting home to his wife and daughter. Although their times together were made more precious by their times apart, they both realized this was no way to maintain a family. Roy often heard himself saying, "I've got to figure out a way to spend more time at home."

One incident in particular gave impetus to that desire. It was February, 1969, and Roy was spending his third week in Hawaii setting up a distributorship. This trip seemed especially long; in fact, Roy had missed his sixth anniversary on January 25, and although Wanda had been understanding, he was still plagued by a nagging guilt.

Since he always felt better when he heard Wanda's voice, he telephoned her now. "Darling, do I ever miss you," he told her.

"Oh, Roy, I miss you too," she said.

They talked for a few minutes; then Wanda put Denise on the line. "She's been jumping up and down to talk to you," Wanda told Roy. "Say hi to Daddy," she told Denise.

In her sweet, practical, four-year-old voice, Denise uttered heart-wrenching words that would imbed themselves in Roy's mind: "Where can I borrow a new daddy?"

That did it. Roy wasn't going to have his family scouting around for a replacement. He wrapped up his business in a hurry and caught the next plane home.

CHAPTER TWENTY-FOUR

While neither Roy nor Wanda was happy about the extensive time he had to spend on the road, they realized his job was a steady one, with a valuable spiritual ministry of its own. In spite of the traveling, they both assumed he would remain forever with Audio Bible Studies. But shortly before Roy's thirtieth birthday, the stage was set for another significant change.

One afternoon, Roy was returning home from a business trip, flying from Chicago to Los Angeles, when he struck up a conversation with the man sitting next to him. The man introduced himself as Ken Opstein, executive vice-president of the Pennsylvania Life Insurance Company. Roy had no interest in hearing about insurance, but the two men took an instant liking to each other. Roy found himself telling about his work with Audio Bible, his methods of hiring, training, and motivating people, and his goals and dreams for the future. Ken listened intently, nodding or making comments from time to time. As they parted company at the airport, they exchanged business cards. "We'll have to keep in touch," said Ken. "Maybe you'd like to think about getting into the insurance business."

Roy grinned good-naturedly; he didn't bother telling Ken that the last thing he wanted to get involved in was insurance. He had been that route before, peddling policies to friends and relatives. "Thanks anyway," he replied, "but I'm happy where I am."

Several weeks later Roy received a phone call from a Bill Dyer, director of executive search for Pennsylvania Life. "Hello, Mr. Comstock," the man said enthusiastically. "We've heard about you and we have an unusual opportunity to discuss with you."

Roy put his hand over the mouthpiece and told Wanda, "It's just some guy trying to sell me insurance. I'll get rid of him." He removed his hand and said, "I'm sorry, Mr. Dyer, but I have all the insurance I need."

"No, no, you misunderstand," came the quick reply. "This is an employment opportunity."

At last Roy agreed to meet with Bill Dyer in a Beverly Hills coffee shop on Wednesday morning. The two talked about Penn Life and about Roy and his plans. "Stanley Beyer, the president of our company, would like to meet you," Bill told Roy before they left.

Roy met with Stanley Beyer, a handsome, dark-haired, congenial man, on Friday morning. He was immediately impressed both by the man and by his plush surroundings. Beyer, a dynamic individual, occupied a vast office boasting paneled walls with shelves containing exotic memorabilia from around the world. The room was furnished with a massive mahogany desk, luxurious couches, Persian rugs, and heavy carved tables with huge lamps.

The secretary had told Roy to go on in and sit down while Mr. Beyer completed a phone call. Roy couldn't help overhearing Beyer's conversation; he was talking to someone in Europe about buying a bank—a half billion dollar deal! Roy swallowed hard and wondered what on earth he was doing in this place; it was one of the rare moments in his life when he had cold feet.

After Mr. Beyer finished his phone conversation, he walked over, closed the door, and locked it. Then he went back to his phone, dialed his secretary and said, "I don't want to be disturbed. I have an important conference going on here. Hold all my calls." Finally he sat across from Roy and said, "You know, Roy, I've heard a lot about you, and I'm excited to meet you."

Roy's first impulse was to look around to see if there was some mistake. Surely Mr. Beyer wasn't talking about *him*.

Beyer was still speaking. "I've heard some wonderful things

about you, Roy, but now I want to hear them from you. Tell me about yourself, everything you've done."

Roy squelched his nervousness and plunged in. He told about his experiences with Kirby, Success Motivation Institute, and Audio Bible Studies; he concluded by stating his goal to become successful in business so that he could underwrite evangelistic work. "I'd like to be able to give a million dollars a year before I'm fifty years old," he said. Even as he spoke, Roy realized he was risking Mr. Beyer's disapproval. How could a Jewish man be expected to sympathize with a goal to win people to Christ?

But Roy had underestimated this unusual man. Stanley Beyer called Roy back for several meetings in the next few weeks. At one meeting he said, "Roy, if you come into this business, I'll make it my personal responsibility to see that you reach your goal."

For nearly three months Roy and Wanda prayed about what they should do. They spent hours discussing the pros and cons.

"There wouldn't be as much traveling with Penn Life," Roy told her one evening as they lay awake, talking in the darkness.

"That's a definite advantage," she murmured.

"There are a lot of success stories in Penn Life, too," he continued. He leaned up on one elbow. "You know, Hon, I've seen that a person can be a success using Christian principles in a Christian organization. But I'm really beginning to feel that God wants me to be a success in a secular atmosphere so that people can see that it's God's power and not just the Christian atmosphere that makes success possible. Do you understand what I'm saying?"

"I think so," she said, easing into his arms. "You're saying that Christian principles will work in a secular situation too, that it's God who works through people, and blesses them."

"That's it, Sweetheart," Roy answered. "I think I know what decision God wants us to make. Are you ready for another major change in our lives?"

Wanda nestled her head against his chest. "I'm ready for whatever the Lord has for our lives, Roy."

On May 15, 1969, Roy joined the staff of the Pennsylvania Life Insurance Company, working out of the home office in Santa Monica under the direction of Stanley Beyer and Ken Opstein. His assignment for the first year was to learn the business and to go out and sell, to prove that he could do it. While he was in training, his standard of living was guaranteed by the company; he received a salary commensurate with, if not better than, what he had earned with Audio Bible Studies.

Roy did a lot of traveling that first year, with a schedule only slightly less rigorous than it had been with Audio Bible. He was sent to Sioux City, Iowa, for part of his training; then for nearly six months he commuted weekly to Chicago, where Penn Life maintained a central office and a division titled "special services." After his training period, Roy was assigned to Birmingham, Alabama, to train salesmen in that special services division. He fulfilled the company's expectations exceptionally well.

Not long after Roy accepted his position with Penn Life, Wanda learned that she was pregnant again. Both she and Roy were excited; they had tried for over three years to have another child. Now they both hoped for a son.

Roy was in Birmingham, Alabama, when the baby's birth drew near. Because he wanted Wanda to be able to reach him at a moment's notice, he carried around an attache phone—a battery-operated, transistorized mobile telephone built into a briefcase. That phone became the object of more than one hilarious incident.

One afternoon Roy was having lunch with one of the Penn Life vice-presidents in the Parliament House Restaurant in Birmingham. Roy had promised to telephone Wanda at a certain time, so he opened the briefcase on the table and proceeded to make his call. As he and Wanda chatted, he became aware of waiters and waitresses hovering around the table, pouring water, offering more bread, peering curiously at his extraordinary phone. Finally Roy's associate reached the limits of his patience. Slamming his fist on the table, he bellowed, "Come on, folks, he's not crazy. He's really talking on the phone. Now get out of here!"

Another time Roy and a salesman entered a coffee shop in a small Alabama town, and sat down. Since there was only one other customer in the place, Roy took the opportunity to open his briefcase and telephone the office for some information. From the corner of his eye Roy spotted the other patron watching him; then the man jumped up suddenly and left. Five minutes later the restaurant was jam-packed with people pressing in around Roy, craning their necks for a look at that magical contraption in his suitcase.

Finally the owner pushed through the crowd and stared skeptically at Roy. "You're crazy, mister," he grunted. "You're not really talking on that thing, are you?"

"Yes, I am."

"All right, then you call me on my number here to prove it," challenged the man.

Roy and the salesman exchanged amused glances; then Roy made the call. When the restaurant telephone jingled shrilly, the owner grabbed the receiver, listened a moment, then hollered excitedly, "Hey, it works! He's talking to me." He waved an excited hand at someone in the crowd. "Zeke, run over and fetch the folks at the phone company. They gotta see this thing to believe it!"

With his mysterious portable phone, Roy was the biggest attraction to hit town in many months.

Roy arrived home just in time for the birth of his son, Michael Brent Comstock, on March 31, 1970. At last Roy and Wanda had the boy they had prayed for—a wonderful, healthy baby.

The day Wanda brought Michael home from the hospital, Roy left for La Costa, a luxurious resort north of San Diego, to attend the company's annual sales convention. At the awards banquet, Roy gazed at the head table where seventeen of the company's top executives sat. Every one of the men at that table was a multimillionaire. Roy asked himself, What did they do in the company to achieve their position and economic status? The answer seemed apparent: Each had gone out and built his own office, his own agency. In that moment Roy decided, *No more running around the country. I've got to have my own office!*

That was just what he told Stanley Beyer when Roy returned to Los Angeles.

Beyer looked Roy in the eye. "Just where do you wish to have your office?"

Roy paused a moment, then replied, "Pennsylvania. The company's charter is in Philadelphia, but since Penn Life moved to California, there are no functioning offices there."

"And you believe this is the best thing for you to do at this time?" Beyer questioned.

"Yes, I do," said Roy. "I want to put Pennsylvania back on the map for our company."

"That's a tall order," mused Beyer. "But go ahead. Call on any of us at any time for help."

On June 21, 1970, with Michael less than three months old, Roy moved his family to Harrisburg, Pennsylvania. Both he and Wanda were excited about their new adventure—and entirely confident of success. They moved into an impressive three-story house which they shared with their new business partners, Keith and Marla Aycock. Keith had been a distributor with Audio Bible Studies, and the two couples had become good friends. Keith had been looking for a new position, so when Roy decided to open his own office, he invited Keith to join him.

They got off to a good start. They hired salesmen, trained them, and sent them out to sell; they both set the pace by going out regularly and selling. Sales were steady, promising. Roy needed the balance Keith brought to the operation. Keith's talents centered in his ability to hit the field every day, while Roy's talents primarily involved management, hiring, training, and motivation. Both men's talents were vital for success, even for survival.

Roy managed his new executive responsibilities very well, except for an occasional small blunder—such as the time during his first sales meeting when he inadvertently misspelled *Pennsylvania* on the huge chalkboard.

Even the living arrangements worked out surprisingly well, considering there were two families under one roof. The foursome accepted their individual differences with a minimum of friction and attempted to accommodate one another's varying schedules. Keith and Marla were night people who liked to stay up late; Roy and Wanda preferred retiring early. The Aycocks ate no breakfast; the Comstocks were early risers who wouldn't dream of skipping that most important meal of the day. Concessions were made on both sides to maintain a pleasant harmony in the household.

Nevertheless, the new venture was short-lived. Three months after the opening of the Pennsylvania office, Keith announced that he was leaving the business. He had acquired a large amount of money from his father and intended to begin a motel management enterprise.

Roy and Wanda found themselves suddenly alone in a sprawling house with huge monthly payments, trying to hold up a fledgling business organization that had just been torn in half. The full burden of both management and sales was now Roy's; it was an overwhelming responsibility. During the next three months Roy and Wanda struggled to keep things going. When they fell behind in their rent, they moved to a townhouse in Hershey, Pennsylvania, and operated the business from there. On numerous occasions Roy received phone calls from his Penn Life associates, offering him help and encouragement. But he refused to admit he needed help. He was determined to make a go of things on his own.

Success grew more improbable with every week that passed. The salesmen were complaining; many were leaving the company. Sales plunged alarmingly. The Pennsylvania office lost money hand over fist. Nearly thirty thousand dollars, all of it Penn Life's money! Stanley Beyer had trusted Roy to be a good steward, to multiply the company's investment. Roy had repaid his faith, his kindness, by unwittingly staging a monumental financial fiasco.

This new failure was a shattering experience for Roy. The day he realized he had to telephone Stanley Beyer and admit defeat, Roy sat for hours brooding over the past, assailed by his old failures and mistakes. His confidence was battered. He was waging a losing battle against depression.

Wanda watched silently and suffered along with Roy. She didn't know what to say or how to comfort her husband. His grief seemed almost too private, too profound, touching the very core of his personality. Her disappointment was great too, but at least her self-esteem wasn't at stake. She knew she would come through this difficult time; she wasn't so sure about Roy.

"We have to talk about it," she told Roy finally.

"What's there to say?" he returned, his expression glum. "I've failed again. It's the same old story."

Wanda sat down beside him and put her hand on his. "I don't believe that. I don't think Mr. Beyer will believe it either."

Roy stared at the floor, his jaw rigid; his gaze riveted in space. "But it's there, Wanda, the pattern of my life. When I was a kid I wanted to be Superman. I wanted it so badly. Do you know how that escapade turned out?"

"No, how?"

"I fell down a hill, broke my arm, and knocked out my teeth." He rubbed his forehead in a slow, ponderous motion. "I've done that all my life, Wanda—chased impossible dreams, then tumbled down hills and knocked out my teeth."

"But you've never stopped trying," she argued tenderly. "That's the important thing."

Roy looked at her soberly. "Is it? All my life I've wanted to show my father I could make something of myself. All I've proved is that I can mess up my life the same as he did."

"All right," conceded Wanda, "so you're like your father in a lot of ways. But you have another Father—and he can help you to be like *him!*"

"I want that," said Roy. "I want that more than anything in my life. But I don't know what God is trying to tell me. Does he want me to give up all the hopes, the dreams?"

"No," said Wanda firmly, squeezing his hand. "I know God gave you the vision to be successful for him, and I know it's going to happen. In *his* way . . . *his* time. We have to believe that. We have to trust him even when we can't understand him."

Roy drew Wanda into his arms. For a moment they clung to each other fiercely, drawing strength from their closeness, their love. "Wanda," Roy whispered into her hair, "would you pray? Pray with me now. I need God's help. I'm nothing without him. I want whatever he wants for us."

They spent the next hour together in prayer. When they finished, Roy telephoned Stanley Beyer. "Stanley, this is hard for me to say," he began haltingly, "but the office here isn't working out. We've accumulated a large number of debts; the salesmen are demoralized. It's just no good. I'm sorry."

Beyer sounded unruffled. "I'll tell you what, Roy. Get on a plane and fly back here. We'll sit down together and talk this whole thing out."

In Stanley's office the next day, Roy had no idea what to expect. Would he be reprimanded? Demoted? *Fired?*

Beyer greeted Roy, then sat down, folded his hands on his desk, and smiled reassuringly. After several moments he cleared his throat and said, "Roy, the reason you're failing is because you're trying to invent the wheel all over again."

"I don't understand," said Roy.

"We in the company know what has to be done and we know how to do it, but you don't want to do it our way. We've all called you and offered our help, but you wouldn't accept it."

Roy gazed pensively at his hands. "I wanted to show you I could do the job on my own."

Beyer stood up and came around to the front of his desk. "Roy, you don't have to prove to us how strong you are. You don't have to be a one-man show. We've all helped one another build this company."

Roy shook his head slowly. "I'm afraid I haven't helped to build anything," he said. "I have no excuse. I just failed—"

"Nonsense," said Beyer. "You have the talent to organize and work with people." He looked closely at Roy. "Do you remember what I told you when you came into this business? I said I'd make it my personal responsibility to see that you reached your goal. But I can't do that unless you do what I tell you. You've got to follow my directions."

"I'm ready to do anything you say," replied Roy.

"Fine," said Beyer. "Go to Sioux City and get back into the special services division where you were trained—and you were training other people. You were excellent at that. You're the best there is."

Roy stared at Beyer with a mixture of astonishment and dismay. "You want me to move to Sioux City, Iowa?"

"That's right. It's our biggest office, number one in the country in sales, production, everything. You'll do extremely well there."

Roy nodded mechanically, but inside he was protesting, *Not Sioux City. That's the last place on earth Wanda and I want to go.* Coming from the Los Angeles area, Roy considered that part of the Midwest *the boondocks.* In fact, at one of his first managers' meetings in Sioux City, he had made the comment, "This isn't the end of the world, but I think I can see it from here."

As Roy left Stanley's office for his flight back to Pennsylvania, he reflected soberly, *So we're moving to Sioux City. Wait'll Wanda hears this!*

CHAPTER TWENTY-FIVE

As Roy and Wanda drove past the city limits into Sioux City, Iowa, in March 1971, they passed the stockyards and a massive pile of fertilizer. Beside that dubious mountain stood a billboard declaring, "Don't let this hill offend you. It represents five hundred million dollars in revenue."

Roy and Wanda weren't impressed. They had few illusions about what lay ahead for them in Sioux City. Roy was literally starting over in the business. Although he was given the impressive title of "Regional Manager for the Midwest," he had to go in and do the job from scratch, prove himself. It was an awesome task, especially for a man whose self-image had so recently been raked through the coals, devastated. Roy's confidence was at a low ebb; without self-assurance, how could he summon the authority to direct and supervise others? Perhaps as never before, Roy was now seeking his confidence in the Lord. Only God could bring the victory for which he and Wanda prayed now with such urgency.

Shortly after their arrival, they moved into a tiny two-bedroom apartment that offered little peace or quiet. Raucous music emanated constantly from the upstairs complex. Curiously, someone overhead also rocked in a rocking chair all day long. Roy and Wanda couldn't escape the persistent *cre-cre-creaking* above them. Fortunately, the apartment was only a temporary dwelling until they could find a house of their own.

In spite of Roy's tenuous self-esteem, he had made a new commitment to success, based largely on Stanley Beyer's faith in him. If Stanley could still believe in Roy after all that had happened, Roy wasn't going to disappoint him now.

Roy knew, too, that he had friends in Sioux City—the people he had worked with during his earlier training period there. Men like Gerry Weiner, Dave Rexius, and Jerry Taylor. Roy could count on their support; in fact, they had called him often in Pennsylvania to offer help and encouragement.

Still, Roy had a difficult time getting started again. His assignment was to create a special services division for selling additional coverage to policy holders. Six other men had been there ahead of Roy, attempting to establish the new division. All of them had failed or been asked to leave.

To begin the new division, Roy was given a half dozen men who had been in what was called the conservation department. However, some of these men were skeptical of Roy, reluctant to recognize his authority. They asked, "Who's Roy Comstock to come in here spouting a fountain of new ideas, stirring things up, telling everyone what to do?" During his first three months in Sioux City, Roy waged a constant battle to get things moving.

Frequently during those early days in Iowa, Roy and Wanda spent their evenings encouraging each other, talking and praying about what God wanted to accomplish through them in this new place.

"We're going to make it," Wanda would assure Roy when he trudged in after an especially demanding day. "Just keep on, Hon. Stanley is behind you. It's going to break through, I know it is."

She was right. One day Roy strode in, his mouth set in determination, and said, "I'm going to take this office to the top, Wanda. In the last month our division's intake has grown tremendously. I sense it's really going to take off now."

"That's wonderful!" cried Wanda happily.

Roy paced the floor, buoyant, propelled by a restless energy. "God has been teaching me incredible things lately," he continued. "I've spent hours studying the Bible, trying to understand just what it says about success and what God wants his children to accomplish in this world. I've learned some amazing things, Wanda."

"I know you've been spending hours every night studying—"

"Yes, and certain facts are becoming clear to me," he replied. "I see the relationship between scriptural principles and the secular principles we use in sales and motivational courses. I'm convinced that God wants his children to be successful. He wants us to be the very best at whatever we do. Nowhere in the Bible does he bless mediocrity. He wants us to step out and dare extraordinary things for him."

Wanda offered a small puzzled smile. "Do you have something specific in mind?"

Roy picked up a Bible from the coffee table. "He wants us to do whatever honors him, whatever utilizes our talents for his glory. Success isn't necessarily making a lot of money, although that may be part of it. Success is making full use of the potential God gave us." He held the Bible out, gesturing with it as he spoke. "It's all here, Hon. We're joint-heirs with Christ of all God's blessings. Think what that means. The earth, the desires of our heart, health, prosperity—*all* things are available through Christ. The problem is our vision is too small. Most people would rather settle for comfort and just enough success to get by."

Wanda smiled in amused agreement. "I'm sure you're right, Roy, but you sound like you're ready to jump up and preach a sermon."

Roy flashed a quick boyish grin. "I'd like to. I'd like to tell Christians everywhere how they can be more than they are— and have more—with Christ's help."

Wanda took his hand and pulled gently. "Can it wait till after supper? The meat loaf is getting cold."

Roy circled her waist with his arm as they ambled toward the kitchen. "This is only the beginning, Wanda," he told her. "I'm putting everything down in a notebook, all I'm learning about godly success. And I'm going to use those principles to make the special services division of Penn Life the best there is."

Roy kept his word. Over the next six months the special services division thrived, going from earnings of several hundred dollars weekly to ten thousand dollars. The "fly in the ointment" was the manager of the former conservation office, the company's number one salesman, who apparently felt threatened by Roy's new position of leadership. Convinced Roy was receiving credit for work he was doing, the man wrote a long letter of complaint to Stanley Beyer and Ken Opstein.

The showdown between Roy and the manager occurred the next year at the President's Club in the Bahamas. Roy's office was number three in the whole country for his division. The manager, because he was the company's top salesman, claimed credit for the division's success. While in the Bahamas, Stanley Beyer told Roy, "The only way you can handle this is to go out and sell and show him where it's at."

"Challenge the top salesman in the country?" mused Roy. "That's a big order."

"I don't think you have any other choice," said Beyer.

Roy nodded thoughtfully. "I'm willing to do that, but here's what I'd rather do. I'll work with the Wichita office for three months. Let our top salesman have the whole office in Sioux City for ninety days. If the business drops, I want it back and I want him out. If he can hold the business where it's at, or increase it, then I'll stay out and never go back to Sioux City."

The next month Roy commuted to the Wichita office, a modest, struggling operation. He sold an impressive total of eighty-two policies. Meanwhile, Sioux City sales plummeted from ten thousand dollars to three thousand for that month. Ken Opstein telephoned Roy and said, "Get back to Sioux City fast!"

Roy returned, knowing at last that he had the full loyalty and support of his men. From then on the division flourished, growing by leaps and bounds. Over the months, Roy polished and refined his growing body of material on success and motivation. He selected several salesmen and worked with them personally, teaching them success principles and observing how they applied them in their lives and work. He saw their work habits improve and their enthusiasm soar. They became the company's top salesmen.

Shortly after the Sioux City office began to boom, Roy and Wanda purchased a nice older three-level home with a pretty fenced backyard, near a school for Denise. Wanda enjoyed redecorating the house—painting walls and having new carpets and drapes installed. The Comstocks would live in this home for twenty-two months—longer than any place they had previously occupied.

This was a pleasant time for Wanda; she was free to stay

home, keep house, care for the children, and go bowling with women of the neighborhood. She and Roy located a good church to attend, and Roy found a rewarding outlet for his evangelistic fervor. He joined the "Flying Ambassadors," an outreach ministry headed by a pilot, Ed Sisam. Roy and Ed traveled throughout the Midwest in a private plane nearly every weekend, preaching in dozens of churches. Life was good and meaningful, for both Roy and Wanda.

Still, they recognized that they didn't want to remain in Iowa permanently. Both held secret hopes that one day soon Roy would be reassigned to California. In fact, Roy's goal was to be promoted to Penn Life's executive level, working out of the Santa Monica home office.

As one step toward that aim, Roy wrote a letter to Norbert Cieslak, vice president in charge of special services, telling Norb he wanted his job and explaining what he would be willing to do to get it. Roy hadn't lost his mind, penning such a blatant communiqué. Actually, the letter was a strategic maneuver. He carefully outlined his plan: Norb had the talent and resources to handle a higher position in the company, explained Roy, but obviously he couldn't step into that niche until he found a replacement. So Roy promised to make the Sioux City special services division number one in the country and assured Norb he would send the most winners to the President's Club. By attaining these goals, Roy would be the logical replacement when Norb was ready to move up.

Norb's reaction to Roy's letter was typical of the company's positive pattern of supporting and encouraging one another. He telephoned Roy immediately and said, "How can I help you reach your goal?"

Roy and Wanda were more than pleased by Norb's response. With support like that, it looked like only a matter of time before they would be heading home to California.

CHAPTER TWENTY-SIX

In December 1971, Roy returned to California—but only briefly and for a totally unexpected reason. Howard Comstock had died.

For some time Howard had been suffering from a leg infection, but he refused to have it treated properly. "The day I go into a hospital, I'll never leave," he insisted. Eventually the infection affected his heart. On Christmas Eve he was admitted to the hospital. As he had predicted, he never came out alive.

Milt was the only family member with Howard when he died—and even Milt didn't realize his father was dying. Of course, Milt was aware of the tubes running in and out of his father's body and the ominous-looking machines and apparatus around his bed. But Howard Comstock had never looked weak or vulnerable, and he didn't look that sick now. In fact, he seemed to have everything on his mind except his own illness.

He looked at Milt and said, "How about you doing me a favor, Curly? I got a lot of guns and stuff in hock. You think you could get them out for me?"

Milt shook his head in sad frustration. "Dad, there's nothing more I can do for you. I'm sorry, I'm broke."

Howard nodded slightly, stone-faced, and replied, "OK, I just wanted to let you know where those guns are."

There was a long moment of silence between the two men; then Howard turned his head toward the television set on the wall. "You know what, Curly," he complained, "they're charging me a dollar a day for that dumb TV over there."

Those were the last words Milt ever heard his father speak. Without warning, without farewell, Howard Orville Comstock was dead.

When Roy arrived in California and met with his brothers and sisters to plan the funeral, he told them he would make the arrangements and take care of the expenses. He brought in his friend, Dr. Paul Cedar, crusade director for the Billy Graham Association, to conduct the services. Roy had met Paul several years before in Omaha, when Paul attended a meeting of the American Evangelism Association. The two men had been stirred by their mutual burden and vision for evangelism, and had kept in touch over the years.

Early on the day of the funeral, Roy took Paul with him to Yucca Valley to pick up some of his father's things. They found a virtual junkyard and a hovel; Howard had lived there in a communal situation with several other older people.

Roy looked around sadly and shook his head. "This was the story of my childhood," he murmured to Paul.

Howard Comstock's funeral turned out to be more a family reunion than an occasion for mourning. All the brothers and sisters gathered with their families in a small chapel in the desert. A strange, warmly nostalgic atmosphere pervaded the room as the offspring clustered around their father's coffin.

Joy whispered to her husband, "I can't understand why I'm not unhappy."

"Because all your family is here," he answered.

Joy nodded and said, "Dad looks so peaceful. The only thing wrong is that he's wearing a suit. He should be wearing his bib overalls."

A moment later, Roy told the small congregation, "My sister Joy has something she wants to read to us. It's a description of our dad. Joy wrote it as an English composition over eighteen years ago."

Joy stood beside Roy and unfolded a worn piece of notebook paper. "When I wrote this, our family had just gotten back together," she explained, "but I didn't want the

kids at school to know Dad had been gone most of my life."
Then in a soft, quavering voice she read, "The rocks crackled
as the pickup truck came up the driveway slowly. It stopped
and the key was turned off. The door opened and a big man
in a red and tan jacket climbed down. The wind blew through
the hair on his almost bald head. His blue shirt brought out
the blue of his eyes. With his black lunch bucket in one hand
and the other hanging at his side, he walked with his long,
easygoing stride toward the house. He hung his coat on the
hook behind the door and stepped into the kitchen. 'Howdy,'
was the deep, thundering sound that came from his lips. He
was a big man of two-hundred twenty-five pounds put into the
height of 6' 3". His face, hands and arms were tan, which was
given to him by the sun during his laboring days. This is the
guy that I kiss good night every night. He is the one that has
been taking care of my brothers and my sisters and myself all
of our lives. He is my father."

After the funeral, as Roy and Milt walked together from the
chapel, Milt struggled to keep his emotions in check. He took
out a handkerchief and dabbed quickly at his eyes, then
furtively tucked it back into his pocket lest anyone interpret
the gesture as a sign of weakness. "I was right there with Dad
when he died," he told Roy, "but I never had a chance to tell
him how I felt about him. I mean, there were things I
respected him for—the way he could make a decision, right or
wrong, and stand up like a man and, if necessary, take the
punishment for it."

"Yeah, I admired that in him too," said Roy.

"You know," continued Milt, "he had pain in his life too, and
he knew he did wrong so many times, and I think he suffered for
it until the end."

Roy nodded, his expression thoughtful. "I feel so many things,
Milt. I've had so many conflicting feelings tied up with that man,
our father. I don't know if I'll ever sort them out."

"There were two things I wanted to tell him," persisted Milt,
no longer looking at Roy. "I wanted to tell him what a blasted
scoundrel he was, bringing so many kids into the world and then
thinking only of himself. And I wanted to say—" Milt's voice
broke, but he pushed on. "I wanted to tell him . . . no matter
what he was . . . I—I loved him!"

In an impulsive, sympathetic gesture, Roy put his arm around Milt's shoulder. Milt—his oldest brother, childhood hero, protector. They walked the rest of the way in silence.

The four brothers—Roy, Ray, Milt, and Bill—rode home together from the funeral in Bill's car. After so many years of going their separate ways, they found much to talk about—the past, the odd twists and turns their lives had taken, their divergent paths. "Do you realize," began Bill, glancing away from the road momentarily, "that the four of us were never together during Dad's lifetime? Oh, sure, we all traveled the hops fields and the spud yards together when we were kids. But since then—in a way we're like strangers."

"You're right," said Milt. "That's one of the saddest facts of our lives."

"Well," said Roy, "if Dad didn't give us anything else, he brought the four of us together now."

"It's just such a shame Richard couldn't have been here, too," said Ray reflectively.

"I can't believe Richard's been dead five years already," added Milt. "Times like now I realize how much I miss him."

"You know," interrupted Bill, his voice suddenly swelling with excitement, "wouldn't it be great if the four of us could live in the same town and do something together, maybe have our own business?"

"You mean sort of make up for the time we've been apart?" asked Milt.

"Yeah, that's the idea."

The brothers looked questioningly at one another. "Roy's the only one who's got anything going for him right now," remarked his twin.

Roy spoke up. "Ray has a point. Things are really moving along for me in Sioux City, so if you guys are serious about getting together, you're welcome to come and look things over and see what you think. I can't imagine anything I'd like better than to have you guys working with me."

In the next six months, all three of Roy's brothers—Bill first, then Milt, and finally Ray—moved their families to Sioux City and became salesmen with Pennsylvania Life. What Howard Comstock had never quite managed in his lifetime was finally accomplished, in part, by his death.

CHAPTER TWENTY-SEVEN

Five weeks before the 1973 President's Club convention, Roy's division had reached second place in the nation, just twenty-two thousand points short of the number one position. Roy told his men, "It's a long shot, but I believe we can catch up and be number one. I'm grabbing a sales kit and going out in the field with you. Let's show the company what we can do!"

During those weeks Roy made the campaign a special matter of prayer. "Lord, it's up to you," he said, "but here's a real chance for us to be number one. It's what I really want—if it's what you want, if you can use it to honor your name."

When the company's top salesmen and managers met in Puerto Rico for Penn Life's President's Club five weeks later, there were fifteen honored winners for the special services division. Twelve of these top fifteen people were from Roy's section. With incredible effort and determination, his office had placed first in the nation for their division.

While in Puerto Rico, Roy talked with Stanley Beyer about the possibility of returning to California. "I think I've done my job in Sioux City," explained Roy. "The office is strong enough to manage without me."

Beyer's expression sobered. "OK," he said slowly, "you replace yourself in Sioux City and you can go back to California."

Roy brightened momentarily; then his smile faded. "You're saying I have to find the right man to take my place and then train him. That could take months, years!"

"Yes, it could," agreed Beyer. "After all, you not only direct the Sioux City office; you're also regional supervisor over seven states. You have your large office, but you also oversee many small ones. That's a weighty responsibility for any man to assume."

"I understand," replied Roy. "But you watch. I'll find the right man. And I'll get to California yet."

The following year was busier than ever for Roy. He was literally driven by the goal—and pressure—to establish his replacement in Sioux City. His office was already in the number one position; now Roy's goal was to double their lead over the second-place office before the next President's Club convention.

With the division prospering, Roy and Wanda moved into a beautiful new house. It appeared that they had attained nearly every cherished dream. They had plenty of money and prestige, a showcase home, the envy of the community. For the first time in their marriage, Roy and Wanda were debt-free; Wanda did not have to work outside the home, did not have to struggle to hold the family together. She was free to enjoy life and take pleasure in her home and children. Since she even had a maid to come in and clean, she found herself with virtually nothing to do. But somehow she didn't feel as happy about her situation as she had expected to.

In fact, she found it increasingly difficult to summon enough enthusiasm to match Roy's exuberance. He was riding a constant high these days; Wanda simply couldn't keep up.

One evening Roy came home and entered the kitchen where Wanda was working, his spirits charged as usual with a special electricity. He kissed her briefly, then paced about, relating the incidents of the day. "The guys are really getting their act together," he said. "Gale Kurtz and Rod Mitchell especially. You know how I've been working with them, teaching them the success principles? Well, they're really doing tremendous work. And, of course, I wasn't sure at first that Gale should even be in the insurance business. But you should see him . . . Wanda, are you listening?"

She looked up distractedly. "What? Oh, yes, I heard you." She glanced away. A voice like a small pinpoint was pricking her consciousness, irritating, but not quite painful. It said, *help*.

"We're doing so well I have no doubt we'll reach our goal of 200 percent above the next office," Roy continued excitedly. "I have a feeling we're really going to knock the socks off the rest of the country. But I couldn't do it without Rod and Gale and the others. Those guys are giving this everything they've got."

Wanda fidgeted with a dish towel, wiping a counter that was obviously already clean. "Roy—" she began.

He helped himself to a glass of milk. "We should have Gale and Jeannie over again soon for dinner, Wanda," he suggested. "You know, I've noticed a real change in them since they became Christians, and I want us to encourage them all we can."

"I'll telephone Jean this weekend," Wanda replied. There was something more she wanted to say, but she couldn't quite focus her thoughts. She needed something, but the need was vague, undefined. "Won't you be traveling in the plane this weekend with Ed Sisam and the Flying Ambassadors?"

"Yes. But we'll be back in time for church on Sunday night."

Wanda looked up. "Then we'll have some time together—?"

"Sure, Hon. In fact, why don't we have Ed and Dorothy over afterward for coffee? It'll give us all a chance to talk."

Wanda reached out imploringly for his arm. "Roy, we need to talk. I need to—"

He looked at her in surprise. "What is it, Wanda? What's wrong?"

She stared at him, her mind suddenly blank. "I don't know," she murmured. How could she describe a feeling that was only a word, a puzzling cry for help.

The telephone rang—it rang a dozen times every evening!—and Roy answered immediately. Soon he was deeply engrossed in conversation.

After church on Sunday evening, Wanda served coffee and cake, then joined Roy on the couch as he chatted with Ed and Dorothy Sisam.

"I've been telling Ed how I'm trying to find a regional manager to replace me," said Roy. He looked back at Ed and grinned. "If anything ever happens in your cookware business, let me know. It would be great to work together."

Ed looked thoughtful. "I'd like to hear more about your company."

Roy drained his coffee and put the cup on the table. "There's no way I could invite you in, Ed, with the idea of your becoming regional manager. You'd have to go out in the field and prove yourself, be the top salesman and earn the respect of the guys, so they'd want you as their leader."

"Be a salesman?" echoed Dorothy. "He's already a regional manager in his business. That would be a step down for him."

Roy nodded. "I can't make any promises, Dorothy, but I think Ed would do very well with us. Why don't we pray about it right now?"

Later, after Ed and Dorothy had gone, Roy put his arm around Wanda and said, "Honey, I'm dead tired. Think I'll turn in. How about you?"

She pulled away. "No, I want to straighten things up first. You go ahead."

He looked at her closely. "Are you feeling OK? You've been so quiet lately . . . so tired."

"I am tired. I don't know why; I don't do anything. If I don't feel better soon I'll call the doctor."

"Good," said Roy, squeezing her shoulder. "Maybe you just need some vitamins."

When Wanda awoke the next morning, the house was silent. Roy had already left for work. Before she even climbed out of bed, Wanda was aware of a gloom, an oppressiveness inside her. It rose like the crest of a wave, nearly choking her. She began to cry.

She got up quickly, wiped away the tears, and stared in alarm at her reflection in the mirror. She looked haggard, drawn, frighteningly pale, her face expressionless. What had she expected—that her image might not be there? A panic welled inside her. It was not rational to cry suddenly, without reason, to lose control. Something was dreadfully wrong.

It had been coming on for weeks—this thing, this dark presence. Depression. "Why? Why me? And why now, of all times?" Wanda said aloud. "For the first time in our lives everything's perfect. Why can't I be happy?"

She went to the window and looked out. The world seemed somehow remote, miles beyond her. She could not touch it; it could not touch her. She hugged her arms against her chest and tried to pray. The words evaporated before they left her lips. Her thoughts churned, confused, incomplete, bombarding one another in her mind. *What's happening to me? I'm falling apart. Everything's hitting at once. All that ever happened to me is rolling in now, drowning me!*

She collapsed in a chair, stunned. *Dear God, who am I? I don't know what to do.* She stared at her hands. They were ice-cold and trembling. Panic gripped her afresh. She needed someone to help her. But whom? Roy was gone so much. And he was so absorbed in business even when he was at home. She had no friends in Sioux City. Neighbors and people at church were still only casual acquaintances. And Mother and Dad were a thousand miles away.

She tried to pray again, but her words were flat and stiff as cardboard. She felt a sudden wedge of guilt. *What kind of Christian am I,* she wondered, *feeling like this?* Abruptly, the tears flowed again.

When Roy arrived home that evening, Wanda made a feeble attempt to express her feelings of confusion and despair.

"I don't feel well," she told him.

"Did you call the doctor?"

"No. I—I made an appointment with Dr. Stuck."

"Our pastor? Why would you want to see him?"

"I don't know, Roy. I just have to talk to someone. I feel so . . . miserable."

"Did something happen today—something to upset you?"

"No, it wasn't today. But something's wrong and it makes no sense and it scares me to death." She began to weep uncontrollably.

Roy took her in his arms and patted her head lightly, affectionately. "There, there, Hon; it's not so bad. Everything's going to be fine, believe me." He held her at arm's length. "Now dry your eyes and listen to this good news. You'll never guess who came into the office today. Ed Sisam. He walked right in and said he was ready to go to work for us. Can you imagine? Of course, I had to do a little talking first. But think what it will mean to the company!"

Wanda wrenched out of his grip and ran from the room. Roy started after her, but the phone rang. One of his salesmen had hit a snag and needed advice, reassurance. By the time Roy finished his conversation, Wanda was already in bed, her face to the wall, apparently asleep.

CHAPTER TWENTY-EIGHT

Wanda kept her appointment and began counseling with her pastor, Dr. Martin Stuck of Central Baptist—a gentle, soft-spoken, gray-haired man in his mid-forties.

"I don't know why I'm here," she confided apologetically during her first visit. "Roy and I have been through so many problems in our marriage, but we finally have it made. We have a wonderful family; his business is a terrific success; he's happier than he's ever been. People keep telling us we've finally 'arrived.'" She paused and sighed heavily. "So why am I crumbling inside?"

Dr. Stuck leaned back in his chair and touched his fingertips together. He smiled kindly. "You say your life is very good now. That's fine. But what's troubling you, Wanda? What is it that hurts?"

Wanda began to cry. "Roy's super busy now," she said. "Even when he's home he's preoccupied with work or he's on the phone." She took out a tissue and blotted her eyes. "He's home physically, but emotionally, mentally, he's a million miles away. We have no real sharing, no communication anymore." She stared at her hands and unconsciously twisted her wedding band. "At least, before," she said hesitantly, "when we were struggling along, we were doing it together, talking and sharing our problems. Roy really needed me. Now . . . now I have nothing to do, no purpose in life."

Dr. Stuck leaned forward slightly. "And that disturbs you very much," he said quietly.

"Yes, yes, of course it does," Wanda replied quickly. "And I—I'm afraid of myself, of my reactions. I have to go to business meetings and parties; I have to entertain because I'm the boss's wife. But it's all a front. I have to pretend because it would be very damaging to Roy's career for him to have a wife who's falling apart. But the effort makes me physically ill."

Dr. Stuck asked slowly, "How do you feel when you're home alone, free to be yourself?"

Wanda's voice grew tremulous. "I feel depressed and angry. I cry, because you see, I'm not free to be myself. I don't even know who I am."

"Well, that's what we're here to find out," observed Dr. Stuck.

The months that followed were a private hell for Wanda, as she slowly, painfully struggled to emerge from the morass of depression that immobilized her. Inevitably she returned home from her counseling sessions, promising herself she would do better, and would keep her emotions in check. But too often her resolves were crushed by an unexpected flow of tears or an angry tirade against the children.

One afternoon when Denise and Michael were a few minutes late arriving home from school, Wanda heard herself screaming, "Where were you? What have you been doing?" The youngsters stared dumbfounded at her; then when Michael, her four-year-old preschooler, protested that they weren't tardy, Wanda grasped his arm and began to spank him harshly. Abruptly she caught herself and, trembling, sent the children to their rooms.

For Wanda, the situation was all too familiar—her temper flaring, the irrational shouting and unwarranted spankings, then the terrible need to escape, to get away, go somewhere, anywhere. Quickly she scribbled a note to Roy. It said simply, "I don't know if I'm ever coming back." She got in her car and, crying all the way, drove the hour-and-a-half trip to Omaha. Over and over she thought, *Huh! Am I ever going to make it as a person?* In Omaha, she tried to calm down by going to see a movie—a nostalgic take-off on the fifties. It only brought more tears. After the movie, she drove to a little motel, checked in nervously, using a credit card, and spent the night crying and praying. The next morning she thought, *Well, I can't stay here.* Wearily, defeatedly, she drove back home.

Roy was waiting for her. "Where were you?" he asked, his voice stern but controlled.

"Omaha," she replied tonelessly. "Good old Omaha. I found a little motel. I don't even remember the name."

"Why? Will you tell me that? In the name of heaven, why?"

"I don't know." She moved slowly, lethargically, removing her coat. "I—I had to get away."

Roy's expression tightened. He spoke with a raw intensity. "When I got home last night, I asked Denise where you were. She said, 'I think Mom took off. She just needed to be alone.'" Roy confronted Wanda and placed his hands firmly on her shoulders. "Wanda, this isn't the first time you've gone off like this. Do you know what it's like not knowing if you're going to be here when I come home?"

She attempted to pull away. "Roy, please, I just don't know how to tell you what's happening to me."

He gripped her tightly. "Is it the business? If it is, I'll get out of it today. If you need to get away from the people and the pressure, if that's what you need—if that's what it takes for me to have you, I'll quit. I won't lose you just to fulfill my goal in business."

"No, no, it's not just the business; it's *me*." She freed herself from his hold and turned away. He followed with the offer of an embrace, but she said quickly, pleadingly, "No, Roy. Please, leave me alone. Don't touch me."

He dropped his hands in exasperation. "Yeah, sure. That's all I ever hear anymore." He was silent for a moment; then, his voice softening, he said, "Do you want to pray together? I know whatever this thing is you're going through, you're going to make it. I trust God for that."

She stared incredulously at him. "Nothing ever bothers you, does it?" she countered in a low, angry voice. "How can you be so strong when we're going through so much? How can you be so happy and easygoing when we've got such problems? I can't cope, Roy. I can't be strong like you. And it makes me feel rotten. How can you do this to me?" The familiar tears erupted once more. "I can't keep up with the pressure, Roy; I can't keep up the front as your eternally cheerful, competent wife. I'm a failure, and I know it!" Before he could reply, she fled out of the room.

In spite of what she said, Wanda wanted more than anything for Roy to help her, to communicate with her. But she couldn't bring herself to reach out to him. She needed that third party, her counselor, to help her. Still, it wasn't until after six or seven months of counseling that she was able to sit down with Roy and share what she was learning about herself.

"I don't know if you will understand," she told Roy quietly after those months, "but I—I guess I reached a place where I realized you had been gone too much of our married life. And there had been too many moves, too many pressures, too many failures. I spent myself trying to hold our lives together, moving from one thing to another, always trying to avoid bankruptcy. Then, suddenly, it looked like we had it made as a family. That is, you had it made in business. But I personally . . . I hadn't made it as a person. Roy, I'm *not* my own person. I can't say anything; I can't do anything; I can't really be myself. You know your purpose in life; now I need to know mine."

Roy attempted a reassuring smile. "Honey, we all have to go through the churning of life to become the person God wants to make of us."

"I know that," said Wanda. "But I can't take people calling us the ideal couple and saying what a perfect, blissful life we lead when all the time I'm collapsing inside. I go to your Saturday morning business meetings and I have to wear a smile and be full of enthusiasm while inside I'm hurting."

Roy replied sympathetically, "Then you don't have to attend the meetings anymore. And I'll cut our entertaining to a minimum. I'll do whatever I can."

The agony was still in Wanda's face. "But there's more. I can hardly sit through a sermon anymore. Dr. Stuck knows all our troubles, and I feel like he's preaching directly at me, saying, 'How come you're having problems? Straighten out your life; be a good Christian; trust the Lord.' "

Roy reached out for her hand and said, "Honey, that just isn't so. He's talking to all of us, not just to you."

"But, Roy, don't you see?" she returned urgently. "My Christianity is on the line. I'm failing not only as a wife and mother, but also in the most important area of my life—as a Christian! That's what hurts the most!"

They gazed at each other for a long moment, sadly, reflectively. Then Roy took her in his arms and held her close. For the first time in months, she didn't pull away.

While Roy kept his promise to Wanda to drastically reduce their social obligations, he could not eliminate from their agenda the company's gala New Year's Eve party in Omaha. Wanda dreaded having to attend. She felt tense; her stomach was in knots; she knew she would be sick afterward. But she went anyway; it was expected.

Wanda managed to cope through most of the evening, offering smiles and greetings and bits of conversation, accepting compliments with an appropriate measure of grace and appreciation, and making small talk with the other wives. But it had been a long time since she had attended a large secular gathering, and the drinking and smoking and partying made her feel more up-tight than usual. There was too much noise, too much confusion; and too many people crowded around, laughing and talking loudly, blowing party horns, and swinging noisemakers.

As the hour of midnight approached, Wanda's dread increased. She knew that at the stroke of twelve everyone would be hugging one another, exchanging kisses. She couldn't tolerate that. Terror rose in her, pounding in her temples; she felt as if her heart would stop in mid-beat. She had to escape. But where? How?

Then the clock struck twelve. *Midnight.* A new year. An explosion of sound and movement and color engulfed her. Then blackness. She swooned. Roy caught her in his arms before she hit the floor.

She opened her eyes, dazed, weak. People were pressing in close, staring open-mouthed. Wanda felt vulnerable, exposed.

She heard Roy say, "She's OK. Everything's all right." Then she saw Milt approaching, offering his arm for support. "Wanda, are you OK?" he asked with concern. "You're white as a sheet."

Desperately she gripped Roy's arm, and Milt's. "Take me home," she whispered. "Please, I want to go home!"

The following days were the darkest Wanda had ever known. She was bound by terror and guilt; the deadly venom of depression had nearly incapacitated her. She could not free herself from the vice-grip of her own dark thoughts. She wanted to die.

She considered suicide. One morning she awoke early and thought, *This is it. I've had it. I'd rather end my life than go on like this.* Calmly she debated how she might accomplish her purpose. She had considered the idea before, idly playing with the possibility in her mind, but now somehow it seemed more real, more plausible. She had come to the end of herself; she was convinced she had failed in every sense. What else was left—except dying?

She got up and stood shakily by the side of her bed, wondering, *How do I do it? Do I take pills or do I slash my wrists?* She stared at her hands, her arms, the smooth, unmarked flesh.

Then, inexplicably, she stopped short. *No, Lord,* she thought suddenly. *I can't do it. I still have Christ.* She fell on her knees and cried out to God as she never had before. "Father, there's still hope as long as I have you. Help me! Forgive me. I can't manage alone. You'll have to do it for me!"

That morning was the turning point for Wanda. In the weeks ahead, she inched her way out of her deep depression; she began to hope; she trusted God to see her through one day at a time.

Through continued counseling Wanda discovered important insights which she was finally able to share with Roy. "Honey, I've learned that I need to be open with you," she told him one evening as she sat brushing her hair. "I need to tell you what I think and feel, even when I don't agree with you."

Roy gazed curiously at her. "Of course, Wanda. I want you to feel you can always be open with me."

"That's just it, Roy. I can't always. I realize now that I've spent a lifetime trying to please others, being overly submissive, doing what I thought other people expected of me—first my parents and then you, Roy. I've rarely voiced my own opinions. In fact, I always felt guilty doing what I wanted or expressing my own wishes. I felt I had to fit everyone else's image of me, conform to their mold. Now I see how wrong that was. I couldn't be the person God made me because I never knew who that person was. I need my own identity, Roy. I need to be my own person."

Roy took the brush from her hand and embraced her tenderly. "How can I help, Honey? What do you want me to do?"

"I'm not sure yet," she answered. "I have a lifetime of habits to overcome. Remember how I used to tell you my parents called me their good little girl? Well, I was taught never to voice my own opinions, never to contradict anything. I wanted my parents' approval so much that I bent over backward to please them. And I've done the same with you, Roy. I worked myself into a box where I was afraid to do anything because I might not measure up to everyone's expectations."

Roy gave her a quizzical smile. "Dr. Stuck made you realize all these things?"

"Yes. I think God worked through Dr. Stuck to reveal them to me."

"So where do we go from here?"

Wanda thought a moment, then said, "Help me to be the person I really am, Roy; help me to find that person. When we make decisions, let's talk things out together. Don't let me sit there and keep my mouth shut and not say anything. Most of all," she added, "be there to listen."

Over the next several months, as Wanda continued working through her deep-seated problems, her relationship with Roy and the children improved immeasurably. She felt happy, confident for the first time in months.

At the same time, Roy's business continued to prosper. The special services division was producing at a phenomenal level compared with other offices, other regions. His salesmen became the pacesetters for the rest of the nation; they went from twenty thousand to eighty thousand dollars of new business weekly.

Periodically Roy traveled around the country with a team of his men, holding what he called "Purpa-Metrics seminars," teaching salesmen and managers the principles for building sales.

At the President's Club convention in April, 1974, Roy's division won by an astounding 300 percent over the second place winner. Ed Sisam was ranked the number two agent for the entire United States and Canada, and number one in Roy's region. He had earned the right to step into Roy's position.

When Roy greeted Stanley Beyer at the convention, Stanley placed his hand on Roy's shoulder and said with a knowing smile, "You can go home now." There was no fanfare, no big announcement, but Roy understood he had just received the promotion for which he and Wanda had worked and prayed with such diligence for nearly three years.

That summer Roy and Wanda said goodbye to their Sioux City friends—Dr. Stuck, Rod and Carol Mitchell, Ed and Dorothy Sisam, Gale and Jean Kurtz, and many others. They returned to Southern California jubilant, their dreams seemingly secure in their pockets, riding a crest of spiritual, personal, and professional victory. Wanda was going home a new person; Roy was returning as Penn Life's top man in the nation. They were practically home free.

CHAPTER TWENTY-NINE

In August Roy and Wanda moved into a house in Lakewood near their home church, where, after a four-year absence, they happily renewed old acquaintances. Because Milt chose to continue working with Roy, he and Armida, his wife of three years, moved to California, too.

With pleasure Roy assumed his new position as national sales manager of the special services division of Pennsylvania Life Company, working out of the Santa Monica home office. Responsible for the sales activities of the company's offices throughout the United States and Canada, he again began to travel extensively.

Accompanied by a specially trained staff, Roy went to the various regional offices, hiring people, setting up training sessions, and laying the foundation for special services divisions across the country.

His major frustration stemmed from the discovery that, while he could teach his success principles so that salesmen could apply them with positive results, those same men could not go out and effectively teach the principles to others. Nevertheless, Roy did an outstanding job of boosting overall sales. When he first accepted leadership of special services, the division was bringing in about one hundred fifty thousand dollars a week nationally. Within two years Roy helped to carry that figure as high as five hundred thousand. He also began to work with the

"instant issue" division, which provided policies that could be
sold to customers on the spot, without being underwritten. This
division soon proved to be a ten million dollar a year business.

Roy's return to Lakewood provided him with opportunity to
reestablish his friendship with Dr. Paul Cedar, who was now
pastor of evangelism at Hollywood Presbyterian Church. Paul
was also president of Dynamic Communications, Inc.
(Dynacom), a low-profile ministry and service organized in 1969,
to reach unchurched people through the mass media. Dynacom
also helps local churches, through seminars, retreats, and
counseling services, to evangelize their respective communities.

Roy had served on Dynacom's board of directors since its
inception. He and Paul recognized their oneness of purpose.
Unashamed of being idealists, they bore the same burden,
cherished the same vision for evangelism. Thus, Roy accepted
the chairmanship of the board and began working closely with
Paul and longtime friend Bob Root, who was Dynacom's vice-
president.

Roy had met Bob Root at the 1963 Billy Graham Crusade in
Los Angeles, when Bob served as executive vice-president of the
Graham Evangelistic Association. Now, under the auspices of
Dynacom ministries, Bob helped Roy fulfill his goal to organize
his success principles into a Christian achievement seminar.
Over the next two years Roy led his "Personal Purpa-Metrics"
seminars in a number of local churches, including his own, First
Baptist of Lakewood. In the seminars he revealed the five
obstacles he believed needed to be overcome in achieving
success: lack of understanding of biblical truths; low self-esteem;
lack of proper motivation; no chosen destination; and lack of
purposeful organization. He related his own story as an illustra-
tion of how even the most unlikely candidate possessed the
potential for success.

"A Christian has the right and the responsibility to be
successful," he told the audience at his Lakewood seminar.
"Christians should be all they can be for Jesus Christ. God
wants to use you to the fullest of your talents and abilities. If you
aren't succeeding, you need to examine your priorities. The
greatest cause of failure is having no goal in life; the greatest
cause of mediocrity is having too many goals of equal
importance. My challenge to you is to be the best at whatever

God has called you to be—and to capture the wealth of the world and give it back to God!"

The more Roy became involved with the ministry of Dynacom, the more he felt that here was the vehicle through which he could channel his money and resources for the work of evangelism. The burden and the vision became clear: to give personal and financial support to Dynacom's evangelistic outreach. As never before, Roy was fulfilling his goals to succeed in business, to participate in a lay ministry through speaking, preaching, or teaching engagements; and to support evangelism.

Early in 1976 Stanley Beyer suggested tactfully that it might be more advantageous for both the company's prestige and Roy's life-style if he moved into a home more in line with his income and position. Beyer actually went house-hunting with the Comstocks. Roy and Wanda were determined to find a house near their home church; they didn't want to lose that spiritual reinforcement and the fellowship of their Christian friends. Within weeks, the Comstocks moved into a beautiful home, not far from Lakewood, in lush Bixby Hills, an exclusive development which visitors could enter only by permission from the guard at the gate.

Once more Wanda heard the familiar comments: *Oh, you're doing so fantastic! You're the perfect couple . . . the perfect family . . . the perfect everything!*

No, we're not, Wanda wanted to protest. *I still am struggling to be my own person. Roy is traveling too much again, and the loneliness is awful. We aren't communicating like we should. Things aren't perfect!*

Roy, too, became concerned about being away from home so much. He was aware of the strain developing again between Wanda and himself, and he didn't have the time he wanted to spend with his children. The kids were growing up so quickly! In many ways, he was a stranger to them.

Determined to avoid the sort of marital crisis they had experienced in Sioux City, Roy and Wanda talked and prayed about what God wanted for them, their family, their work, their ministry.

"I've been doing a lot of thinking lately," Roy told her one evening as they sat talking together in their den after the children had gone upstairs to bed. "I'm concerned about our closeness as a family. I know my traveling is putting too much pressure on you, and I realize I don't see enough of the kids."

"I've felt that way for quite a while now," Wanda admitted.

"Yet I feel the quality of our time together is more important than the quantity," said Roy.

"But even the quality has been down lately," Wanda told him. "And I can't take sitting around the house all the time while you're on the road."

"So what do we do about it?"

"I've been thinking about going into real estate," said Wanda.

"You, selling houses?" Roy asked, surprised.

"It's something I've thought about for years," Wanda replied. "I need to accomplish something on my own, or I'll slip back."

"Then do it," said Roy. "Take the classes, whatever's involved."

Wanda looked doubtful. "People might think I'm crazy, working when we have everything we could ever ask for."

"Who cares what people think . . . as long as it makes you happy?"

"But it still doesn't solve our problem of finding more time to spend together as a family."

"No," agreed Roy, "but what would you say if I told you I was going to stop traveling so much?"

"Stop traveling? Are you serious?"

Roy nodded. "I'm beginning to feel the Lord is leading me away from the corporate life."

"I don't understand," said Wanda. "This has been your dream, being on the executive level."

"Yes, I know," said Roy. "I used to imagine someday becoming president of Penn Life. I even thought maybe it could give me a platform for my ministry—you know, the credentials, the influential position to speak to the world about Christ. But then I realized I would be getting away from my real goal, the burden God has given me since our days in Minnesota."

"You mean to support evangelism? But you're doing that now."

Roy's gaze drifted over the room as he carefully formed his thoughts. "You see, as an officer of the company, you're limited to a specific salary. Granted it's a good one, with lots of benefits. But as an *agency owner* I could build assets and own residuals. So the real potential for income is in running my own agencies, owning a percentage of the profits."

"But doesn't that mean being a regional manager again, like you were in Sioux City?"

"That's right, Honey," Roy replied. "Except that I wouldn't be stepping into the company's largest office. I'd be starting my own office—not just a new division—from the ground up."

Wanda's expression reflected the seriousness she saw in Roy's eyes. "It would be a risk," she said.

"It would be a way for God to accomplish his purpose for my life and for us as a family," he returned with a smile. "And just think. I would be working regular hours instead of traveling all week."

Wanda's eyes brightened perceptibly. "You mean, you'd be going off to work every morning and coming home every evening for dinner?"

"Most of the time," answered Roy.

"I wonder if we could stand it—seeing so much of each other?" Wanda laughed.

"But I'd still be very busy building a regional office from scratch. It would require real commitment and dedication from both of us. And," he added thoughtfully, "for me it would mean giving up the plush office, the fancy hotel suites, access to the company jet, the title and prestige, that whole ambience of executive status."

Wanda met his gaze. "It's been a hard climb, Roy. Are you prepared to give all that up?"

Roy reflected for a moment, then said, "Yes, because the potential is greater out there with the agencies. The sky's the limit. And eventually I would have more freedom—time for you and the kids, time for the seminars and preaching engagements. I believe God will bless us as a family and bless our service for him if we dare to step out and act on our convictions." He paused, then added, "But I won't do anything, Wanda, unless you, too, feel it's right for us."

"Where would you have your office . . . your agencies?" she asked.

"I don't know yet. I'll have to talk with Stanley."

Wanda was silent for a time; then she said, "I'm ready to go wherever you go, Roy. God has been so good to us. I want whatever pleases him."

One evening a few weeks later, Roy strode in the door after work and, with unexpected exuberance, swung Wanda up in his arms. "We've found the spot," he told her excitedly.

She wriggled free and stared at him in bewilderment. "What are you talking about?"

"We've found it. The place to build an office!"

Her face flushed slightly. "Where? Tell me!"

"San Jose, California," he replied.

Her face betrayed dismay.

"Wanda," he said, "market research figured it would be the best area. It's fastest growing in population; it's the best area economically; and the people are receptive. In fact, Stanley wants the office to be a training center where people can come from all over the country to learn the business. That way, they can visualize and experience the operation firsthand."

"But San Jose? I still don't see why—"

"It's the ideal training ground, Wanda—close enough to San Francisco to be metropolitan and close enough to Fresno and the farm country to be rural. Actually, I'll build the regional headquarters in Santa Clara; and the company already has branch offices throughout the northwest."

"So this is it then," reflected Wanda. "We'll be leaving our families, our friends, our church, and moving to San Jose."

"It looks that way," said Roy. "Can you believe it'll be our twenty-fourth move in fourteen years?"

"Oh, yes," she said quickly, laughing, "I can believe it!"

"And guess what!" Roy continued eagerly. "I'm taking my entire staff up there. Milt will be going with us. And maybe Bill too. We'll have family with us after all."

Roy and Wanda's move to San Jose was prefaced by a rare, wonderful, unexpected experience. They witnessed the miraculous answer to Bertha's prayer for her oldest son. Roy had never forgotten his promise to his mother, so from time to time over the years he had talked to Milt about Jesus. Milt had always listened politely but had never demonstrated any interest in making a personal decision for Christ.

Then in December, 1976, Milt spent a weekend with Roy and Wanda to discuss his move to San Jose. Roy was scheduled to speak on Sunday at a men's retreat at Forest Home in the San Bernardino mountains, so he invited his oldest brother to go along. Milt said OK.

The night before the retreat, in their upstairs bedroom, Roy and Wanda knelt and prayed fervently that God would speak to Milt's heart in the service the next morning, and save him.

While they prayed, Milt lay awake on his pull-out bed in the den directly beneath them. Suddenly, a voice pierced his consciousness, urging, "Milt, get on your knees and pray."

"For what?" Milt said aloud in baffled astonishment.

"It's time now," the voice said, penetrating his mind again. "It's time for you to find Jesus; it's time for you to open your heart and find Christ."

Milt still didn't understand. He shook his head, confused.

Then the voice commanded, "Milt, get down on your knees and pray!"

In the moment that Milt obeyed and fell down on his knees before God, he knew the decision was made, sealed forever. Christ was his. He felt relief; the burden was lifted; he had peace inside.

The next morning as Roy and Milt drove up to Forest Home, Milt was silent; he didn't know how to express what had happened to him. When Roy spoke in the Sunday school hour, and later when evangelist Ginger Kelly gave a stirring message in the church service, Milt listened intently. For the first time he really understood what he was hearing. On their way down the mountain, Milt said, "You know, Roy, I have something to tell you. I didn't raise my hand when they gave the invitation today, but I prayed that same prayer last night."

Roy was elated. He and Milt talked for a while; then Roy said, "The best thing to do is to share your experience with somebody."

When they arrived home, Milt said to Wanda, "Do you believe in prayer?"

"Of course," she replied.

Milt smiled merrily. "Well, I know my mother prayed for me, and you've been praying for me. I want you to know I have Christ in my heart."

That afternoon Milt telephoned his wife Armida with his news; she had accepted Christ two years earlier at a women's retreat. Then he telephoned his brothers, Bill and Ray, and told them of his decision. Finally, that evening at Lakewood Baptist, when Roy introduced Milt to his pastor, Dr. James Borror, Milt's first words of greeting were, "Did you know? I just accepted Christ!"

.

CHAPTER THIRTY

A new location, another beginning. The lush Santa Clara Valley. Early in 1977 the Comstocks moved into a sprawling Spanish-style home in Los Gatos, nestled in the Santa Cruz Mountains. Twelve-year-old Denise and seven-year-old Michael were enrolled at Valley Christian School, and the family began attending Calvary Baptist Church of Los Gatos. Wanda, having successfully obtained her license, began her career in real estate. Roy opened his new office—a modest one at first—and began the arduous task of building a thriving business with little more than sheer faith, a handful of time-tested principles, and a small, loyal staff. Unofficially, he had taken responsibility for the northwest region of Penn Life Company and its subsidiaries, Trans Pacific Insurance Company and Executive Fund Life Insurance Company.

Immediately his salesmen hit the streets, going door to door and writing "Safe Driver's Plan" insurance policies under the instant issue division. Roy began recruiting, hiring, and training additional salesmen, anywhere from four to eleven new people a week. After a few months, the agency had grown sufficiently to warrant a move into a larger set of offices in an attractive modern building. Roy's staff had swelled to over fifty-five agents. His goal was to establish seventeen offices in Northern California within two years, and to open thirty-five new offices in the northwest region.

But Roy's goals centered on more than business. He had come to the San Jose area with the resolve of giving greater priority to his family. He was convinced that finally he and Wanda would be able to create a truly consistent home life— dinner together in the evenings, a regular family routine, a chance for Roy to share in the day-to-day activities of his children.

But it was easier said than done. The demands of starting a new business were incredible, draining Roy's energies, devouring countless hours. And old work habits were nearly impossible to break. For Roy, it was an agonizing struggle to keep priorities in order, to prevent endless business obligations from smothering the precious family life he and Wanda were nurturing. Wanda, too, found her new realty career unexpectedly overwhelming. To be successful, one had to devote full time to cultivating clients, following leads, and showing homes and properties during evening hours as well as by day. Finally, for the sake of her family, Wanda abandoned hopes for a career in real estate.

By midsummer, Roy had to face two disturbing facts: the agency was not expanding as swiftly as he had anticipated; and several of the key people he had expected to assume positions of leadership simply did not work out. The company maintained a policy that a leader had to be able to sell forty policies a week, to demonstrate to trainees the potential for sales and income. Experience had revealed that most new salespeople were satisfied to do half the business of their trainer. Thus, leaders had to keep their sales consistently high. One of Roy's most difficult tasks was dismissing managers who couldn't make the grade.

But where some failed, others stepped in with amazing ingenuity and persistence. Milt's wife Armida, who had worked in the Sioux City office, served as Roy's office manager in Santa Clara, and did an outstanding job. While the agency wasn't growing by leaps and bounds, it was pushing forward at a slow but steady rate.

Still, Roy wasn't satisfied. He wanted to see greater progress. He threw himself into his work, spending every available moment at the office or in the field. Once again he became oblivious of his wife and family. In an effort to do everything himself to make his business succeed, he was no longer relaxing in God or trusting him for his success. Wanda, reacting to Roy's lack of attention, began to withdraw within herself again; she became introspective, sullen, unhappy. Feeling unnecessary and unloved, her rosy visions of a blissful family life dissolved. Then God brought the two of them up short. His Spirit pricked their consciences, nudged their wills, urged them to put Christ back in first place. Together they went forward at a Sunday morning service to renew their commitment to God and to their marriage.

Today Roy says, "Satan's attacks are greatest in times of greatest potential. The way Satan always gets to me is through my pride. I begin to feel I can 'do it myself.' Then I have to reach the place of facing myself and admitting I need God's power."

Roy and Wanda may face more ups and downs than most people because they are not content to sit back and live ordinary lives; they insist on striking out, pushing themselves to the limit, stretching their muscles to reach seemingly unattainable goals, daring and risking the impossible.

Both Roy and Wanda continue to be excited about what God is doing in their lives. Wanda says, "I feel we have every material thing we could ever hope for. Yet, if he takes it all away we will still be able to survive, and we will still be able to go out and do it again. Because of our past failures and successes, I think we can probably handle just about anything that could happen.

"I'm still not wild about entertaining," she adds with the trace of a smile, "but I'm getting better. What's important is that Roy and I know our weak areas. We know where we're vulnerable. We realize we can't manage without the Lord. He blesses us financially, but he also blesses us by making us stronger Christians."

Roy admits that many of their problems have come because he hasn't disciplined himself to leave business behind and concentrate on his family when he is at home. "The key isn't necessarily spending more time at home, but in knowing how to change hats, how to be a husband and father. You can't be a corporate executive with your family." This is a lesson Roy confesses he is still learning.

One of the rewards of making the family their new priority

is that Roy is becoming more than superficially acquainted
with his children. Michael and Denise, both Christians since
early childhood, are blond, slim, gentle-spirited youngsters;
they are polite, almost shy, around visitors. With their parents
they are receptive and obedient. They don't consider their
folks especially strict.

In second grade Michael earned straight A's; his favorite
subject was science. Being "all boy," he loves soccer. For a
small weekly allowance he is expected to take out the trash,
make his own bed, and clean his room. Both children tithe
their allowance and have their own church envelope and
number. At seven, Michael, considering a three-cent tithe a
rather paltry sum, often tosses in his entire thirty-cent
allowance.

Denise, a teenager now, likes to read, listen to music in her
room, and spend time alone thinking. She plays the piano and
likes roller-skating and horseback riding. And she dreams of
someday becoming an actress with her own TV show. When
she became a teen Denise received a dollar a week allowance.
Like Michael, she is expected to make her own bed and keep
her room clean. On Sunday and Monday, the days the
housekeeper has off, Denise is in charge of dishes and other
minor tasks around the house. To earn extra spending money,
she pulls weeds, cleans the patio, or baby-sits for a neighbor.

Admitting she finds it easier to talk to her dad than to her
mom, Denise says, "I can talk to Mom about homework; with
Dad I can talk about boys and things. I can tell Dad anything!"
To help cultivate this attitude of sharing between father and
daughter, Roy takes Denise out on a dinner "date" every year
for her birthday, a tradition he has followed since she was
eight.

With the aim of nurturing a spirit of closeness and
togetherness, the Comstocks are attempting to set weekends
apart as a family time. Friday nights belong to Roy and
Wanda; they go out to a restaurant for dinner, attend a
concert or a play, or spend a quiet evening at home.
Whenever possible, Saturdays revolve around the children.
Roy, Wanda, and the youngsters may go roller-skating or bike
riding, or if there is a good movie on "TV home box office,"
Wanda may make a heaping bowl of popcorn, bring out the

Pepsi Lite, and join the family around the television set.

Sunday mornings and evenings are reserved for church, where Roy teaches a single young adults Sunday school class. On Sunday afternoons the Comstocks go out for dinner, visit with friends, or have a backyard barbecue. Roy and Wanda may walk down to a nearby lake brimming with fish and ducks, or follow the narrow, intimate trails in an adjoining woods, for a few special moments of privacy, of talking and sharing. On warm, sunny days, the Comstocks may swim or relax around their pool, enjoying the breathless, panoramic view of the valley.

Recently Roy purchased a van so that the family could participate in more recreational activities. To try out the new vehicle, Roy and Michael drove to Turlock Lake Reservoir for a private weekend together. It was a rare time of communion and sharing between father and son. They hiked, swam, made boats out of sticks, played kick-the-can, and dug themselves a "lake" on the beach. On Sunday morning they had their own miniature church service in the van, with Michael reading from the Bible and Roy praying—a sun-washed, ragtag congregation of two.

As part of Roy's attempt to instill some tradition in his family, to give his children a sense of continuity and heritage, he and his brothers have created their own coat of arms, with an appropriate symbol for each brother. Roy's symbol is the owl, representing wisdom (both his office and their home contain collections of owl replicas). Milt's symbol is the helm's wheel of a ship, for guidance; Bill has the lion, for strength and endurance; and Ray has the thoroughbred horse, for breeding and quality of life.

Despite differences in personalities and life-styles, the four brothers maintain close ties. Of the four, Bill, Milt, and Roy still work together for Penn Life. Bill is personnel manager in the Santa Clara office; Milt helped establish Roy's office, but following a recent promotion, he has begun traveling to offices throughout the United States.

Roy's efforts to establish a sense of continuity for his family are perhaps best accomplished by their daily routine of living. Weekdays follow a familiar, agreeable pattern. Roy gets up at six A.M. and exercises. (Sometimes Wanda and the children jog with him around the neighborhood.) Around seven, following a shower and a time of Bible study, Roy goes downstairs where the housekeeper has breakfast on the table. By seven-thirty, Michael and Denise are ready for school, so Roy drops them off at the bus stop before making the fifteen-minute drive to work.

He likes to arrive at the office before anyone else so he can check his schedule and get organized, although he finds it almost impossible to beat Milt, who is usually there with the coffee ready. By eight A.M., Armida and several others arrive for a managers' meeting, to discuss current problems and methods for aiding any floundering salesmen. Shortly before ten the salespeople begin to arrive. They cluster in small, amiable groups, drinking coffee, helping themselves to a tray of cookies, and talking over their latest coups or crises. A few are first-timers, invited to sit in on the sales meeting and afterward to be interviewed by Roy.

The sales meeting, which begins at ten, boasts the atmosphere and enthusiasm, the energy and fervor, of a combined pep rally and evangelistic crusade. Against a backdrop of splashy posters advertising the upcoming President's Club, approximately fifty agents shout cheers with the guileless excitement of school children. "We're number one! We're number one!" they bellow in unison. Roy leads them grandly, with the precision and passion of a cheerleader.

Then come the testimonials. Roy announces the agents who made the most sales for the week, then invites each one to the front to share his *fait accompli*. The winners are treated to rousing cheers; the rest are challenged to "go forth and do likewise." Having received a strong dose of inspiration and motivation, the agents go to their assigned territories, bent on making sales.

Following the sales meeting, Roy holds a personal interview with each prospective agent. Sitting back casually in his chair, but speaking with an unmistakable authority, Roy inquires, "Why do you want to get into sales? . . . What sparked your interest in our company? . . . What are your dreams . . . your daydreams? . . . What about the long hours involved in selling?" He always warns possible salespeople, "The hardest part about our business is the rejection, constantly hearing someone bawl, 'No, I don't want that. Get off my porch!' Success depends on how well you keep going in the face of rejection. You have to have a good idea of your goal and purpose in life to be willing to hear that constant *no*. And you have to be willing to do just what I tell you," he adds meaningfully. "I don't want my agents trying to invent the wheel all over again."

On a certain day in February, 1978, Roy interviewed two men. One he hired; the other he turned away. The first interviewee was a young black man, soft-spoken, earnest, almost reticent, who had had no previous experience in sales. The second prospective agent was a talkative middle-aged man with an extensive background in sales and in teaching motivational courses. He was friendly, confident, and aggressive; clearly an extrovert.

Surprisingly, Roy hired the first man and turned away the second. "The reason is simple," he explains. "The first man is teachable, eager to learn. I don't want anyone in the business unless I feel I can contribute to his growth, help build his life. I look for 'ordinary' people. If they've been in insurance before, I probably won't hire them." He continues, "I put new agents through a program of personal tutoring, classroom training, and field experience before they are licensed by the state. And I won't allow anyone on the street to sell until I've seen and approved his presentation."

Roy usually has contact with his salespeople three times a day—at the morning sales meeting; at lunch when everyone meets together at a local coffee shop; and, on Monday through Thursday, around nine in the evening, when Roy returns to his office to receive their telephone reports. Often, he spends the afternoon and part of the evening going out to the field with his men, helping them, instructing them, evaluating them.

When Roy is home for dinner, he arrives around five, shortly after Wanda and the children. Recently Wanda found a satisfying position as placement director for Sawyer Business College in Santa Clara. The work is giving Wanda further opportunity to develop her own identity, to work with the public and help people, and to overcome her natural reticence around others.

Sometimes Roy and Wanda have a few minutes to share the day's happenings before the housekeeper serves dinner. After the meal, while the housekeeper clears the table and does the dishes, the family remains at the table for a time of devotions.

Using the *Bread of Life* booklet or *Family Life Today* magazine, each member reads and discusses a portion of Scripture for that particular day. The evening is usually a relaxing time for the family, providing a couple of hours to talk, read, or watch TV before Roy returns to the office for his agents' calls.

Presently Roy's goal is to build the Santa Clara office into a "power base" successful enough to be used as a model operation for other offices. While his office is still too new to be a President's Club winner, it is rising quickly on the charts. In fact, Roy was able to send three winners to the 1978 President's Club.

At this writing, Roy's office is chalking up about six hundred applications weekly. Roy's dream is to create a sales organization that writes ten thousand instant issue applications a week. Roy says, "Because of the foundation and structure we have, it's just a matter of numbers now, of getting enough people; it's all mathematics from here. We know we can do it in about ten years. There's no question in my mind. The principles I believed in and followed and held on to, no matter how tough things were—they work, they proved true."

Roy currently owns agencies throughout the Northwest. Twenty of his closest associates are multimillionaires; it appears likely that, in time, Roy will join their ranks. He intends to fulfill the vision he believes God gave him as a struggling young evangelist in Minnesota.

Because Roy's desire to participate in evangelism still runs strong, he speaks frequently in churches, at retreats, and in Christian Businessmen's meetings. Recently he had the rewarding opportunity to pray with Milt's stepson when the youngster came forward to accept Christ. Milt comments, "That sort of thing is Roy's life. I'm thankful to have had a mother who had a son like Roy."

Roy is also involved in the local chamber of commerce, serving on the governmental relations committee of Santa Clara, and he has been to the state capitol to meet with senators regarding various insurance laws. He was also urged to run for the United States Congress in the 1978 election, but he declined the invitation in favor of his present priorities.

On a recent Sunday evening, Roy preached in his home church, Calvary Baptist, where Pastor Blaine Bishop welcomed him to the pulpit. Roy spoke frankly, personally, of his childhood and youth, and his salvation experience. Then he talked of the pressures on his home and family today. As he gave the closing invitation, Roy asked Wanda, Denise, and Michael to join him at the altar in a public demonstration of their own pledge of solidarity as a family before God. Roy invited others who shared that prayer and commitment to come forward and stand with them. Quietly, prayerfully, with tears and embraces, couples and families came. It was an exquisite moment for Roy and Wanda, who know intimately the pain and the price of the maturing process in a marriage.

Today, the Comstocks wish they could say they have found all the answers, solved all their difficulties. But they can make no such claim. Roy and Wanda know they have by no means arrived at a problem-free level. Even having their lives put down in a book has added another pressure. During a recent clash, Wanda demanded, "Who are we to have a book written about us? We have problems just like everybody else."

Yes, problems. At times, seemingly overwhelming problems. But through it all, both Roy and Wanda refuse to let loose of the commitment they have made to God and to each other. They refuse to succumb to the alarming trend, even among Christians, of giving up on their marriage when the going gets tough.

Through the years, the Comstock men have demonstrated an intense loyalty, a rare, unswerving devotion to one another. At the same time, they have shown a deep-rooted tendency to take women for granted, to discount their importance in their lives— whether the woman is their mother, sister, or wife. This was the inclination of Howard Comstock toward Bertha, and the trait has resurfaced in several of his sons. The tendency is there to hold in high esteem that which is masculine, aggressive, strong, competitive. This subconscious tendency, which Roy says he has only recently begun to recognize in himself, may have been shouting volumes to Wanda through the years of their marriage, reinforcing the negatives in her own faltering self-image.

Both Roy and Wanda realize they are dealing with lifelong habits, patterns of thinking, of acting and reacting, ingrained behavior, and conditioned responses nurtured from their earliest days of childhood. They recognize unashamedly that were it not for Christ in their lives, their marriage would have ended long

ago. They likely would not have tolerated the divisive—and abrasive—traits of character in their divergent personalities.

But they are convinced God has chosen them for each other, that he has made them one in him to demonstrate his power in the lives of his children. By imbuing them with greatly contrasting personality traits and seemingly volatile and unresolvable problems, God daily manifests his "holding" power—teaching them, revealing insights, and molding their characters in the image of himself. It is not always an easy lesson for either of them, but it is meaningful and vital and profitable in ways that they are only beginning to fully comprehend.

Their message to Christian couples is not that they have solved all their problems and reached some sublime apex, a level of perfection that obliterates friction and stress. No, their message is more realistic than that. It is that no matter what the struggles, the clashes, or the conflicts, Christ is always there—his Spirit in them, supportive, wooing, revealing truths, directing their impulses and responses.

Both Roy and Wanda attribute their salvation, their successes, and their sanity to Christ. There are times, of course, when, yielding to pride, they turn deaf ears to God and to each other. Those are the occasions when God prompts them back and reminds them that the key to marital and spiritual success is in daily keeping the channels of communication wide open with Christ and with each other.

To Roy and Wanda, the future represents both a promise and a challenge. A promise of new opportunities for witness and service and giving. A challenge to be all they can be—for each other and for Christ's glory, so that those who watch their lives may see an example of God at work in a contemporary home and family.